RECOVERY

Freedom from Our Addictions

Russell Brand

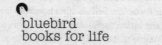

bluebird
books for life

First published 2017 by Bluebird
First published in paperback 2017 by Bluebird

This edition first published 2018 by Bluebird
an imprint of Pan Macmillan
20 New Wharf Road, London N1 9RR
Associated companies throughout the world

www.panmacmillan.com

ISBN 978-1-5098-5086-0

135798642

A CIP catalogue record for this book is available from the British Library.

Designed and typeset by Andrew Barron @ Thextension

Printed and bound by CPI Group (UK) Ltd, Croydon, CR0 4YY

Visit www.panmacmillan.com to read more about all our books
and to buy them. You will also find features, author interviews and
news of any author events, and you can sign up for e-newsletters
so that you're always first to hear about our new releases.

To Laura Kate Brand, for bringing me home

Contents

Acknowledgements

Firstly I acknowledge Bill W, the founder of 12 Step fellowships, a drunk, a madman and a prophet who had the foresight and humility to make this an 'anonymous' program. Somehow he and his co-founders were able to wrangle their leviathan egos in order to perfectly establish this phenomenal template.

I acknowledge all the drug addicts and alcoholics who have helped me in my own recovery, too many to name or even rightly remember but to whom I am forever indebted and connected.

Starting with the singular and magnificent Chip Somers and including some giant souls, flawed incendiary, gentle savages, wild sages. Alfie, James, Sadie, Sandy B, to name but a few, room after room of casual, holy eloquence. Noreen Oliver, a Chanel-wrapped saint with a flick knife in her pocket.

Peggy, the octogenarian gangster, dispensing love like moonshine, Monica, her sidekick – everyone at Friendly House.

My Wednesday friends, Deano, Uncle Rod, Richard, Mark, Simon, Brian, Will, Steve, Rick, Sam, Leon, Vernon, Jeff, Jake, Damo and of course Nik.

My mates who walk the path with me – Sy the sulking siddhu, Jeff, James, Perry.

Jason, my dear friend and brother but 'only in the world ...'

My silent partner, thanks for riding shotgun and not firing too often. Thanks for the crosses in from the right, providing Andy Carroll balls to get on the end of.

Bobby Roth, my dear brother further down the transcendent pathway, thank you.

Radhanath Swami, for guiding me out of the swamp. Hare Krsna.

Jimmy M, mentorship, classical wisdom via Goodison Park. Intense grace, 'enlightened self-interest', constantly quoted and appreciated. Thank you.

Meredith and Wainwright, The Churchills: ... 'I adore you both, Roshis, Wisdom at the point of a pin.'

Tim M, compassionate assassin, compiler and composer of much of the material in this book, especially the worksheets and the formula for Steps 4–10.

Herb K for his book *Twelve Steps to Spiritual Awakening*.

Patrick Carnes.

All the perverts and malcontents I've been in treatment with. The counsellors and mental health professionals. Jackie. Sam. Tony. Travis.

All the various editors and collaborators that have helped me as a writer. Ben Dunn, Byngo, Fran, Martino Sclavi, John Rogers.

Gareth Roy, a tiger behind the lens, guiding me gently.

Jengo.

Nicola Schuller, Sharon Smith, my dear sisters.

Karl Theobald, for the ongoing contributions to my worldview. Working. Class. Hero.

Matt Morgan, for the pricking and goading.

Gee, for Jedi nights.

Adam Venit, a big Hollywood agent with an unHollywood heart. He is one 100 per cent real for his 10 per cent.

Simon, Jessica and all at WME.

9

My new management team: Hannah Chambers, who uses 'the finger' and 'fuck you' as unthinking negotiation tools. Charlie, Katy, Sophie, George. Thanks.

Bev James, who is devoted and potent and authentic. Who has worked on this book on faith alone, thank you.

All at Pan Macmillan, Jodie and Hockley, and Gillian in the Flat Iron citadel.

And dear CarolA, who began as a stalking horse, to drive negotiation with another publisher, but with elegant tenacity, with fluid and feminine passion became my partner on this book. Gentle strength, exactly what the world needs. Thank you.

Introduction

Here in our glistening citadel of limitless reflecting screens we live on the outside. Today we may awaken and instantly and unthinkingly reach for the phone, its glow reaching our eyes before the light of dawn, its bulletins dart into our minds before even a moment of acknowledgement of this unbending and unending fact: you are going to die.

You and your children and everyone you love is hurtling toward the boneyard, I know you know. We all know but because it yields so few 'likes' on Facebook, we purr on in blinkered compliance, filling our days with temporary fixes. A coffee here, an eBay purchase there, a half-hearted wank or a flirt. Some glinting twitch of pleasure, like a silvery stitch on a cadaver, to tide you over. And you're probably too clever to 'repose in God', or to pick up some dusty book where the poetry creaks with loathing for women, or gays or someone. Maybe if quantum physics could come up with some force, or web, or string or something that tethers the mystery to something solid, something measurable, you'd think again but until then there's nothing but an empty grave and a blank tombstone, chisel poised. So no one's going to blame you if you perch on a carousel of destructive relationships and unfulfilling work, whirling round, never still, never truly looking within, never really going home.

Because I had 'the gift of desperation' because I fucked my life up so royally, I had no option but to seek and accept help. Since being relieved of the more obvious manifestations of my incessant drives and appetites, I have paced backwards like a flunky leaving the Queen through a series of less obvious, and not lethal, but still bloody uncomfortable addictions. I believe that what the 12 Steps and their encompassing philosophy, which I will lay out for you in these pages, will provide is nothing less than a solution to the dissatisfaction of living, and dying, to anyone with the balls to do the work. And it is work. Indeed it is a personal rebirth and the journey entails all manner of uncomfortable confrontations with who you truly are. Be honest, have you ever sat down and inventoried all of the things that bug you: the childhood skirmishes; seething stings of patricidal rage; your fury with the government or traffic or global warming or racism, or Apple for continually changing their chargers? When are you planning to become the person you were born to be? To 'recover' your connection to an intended path? On holiday? When the kids leave school? When you get a pay rise? Tick-tock, tick-tock, chisel poised.

I am not writing this book because I think I'm better than you. I know I'm worse. I have spasmed and spluttered through life motored by unconscious drives, temporally fixing in a way so crude and ineffectual that the phenomenon is conveniently observable. The condition in extreme is identifiable but the less obvious version of addiction is still painful, and arguably worse, because we simply adapt to living in pain and never countenance the beautiful truth: there is a solution.

We adapt to the misery of an unloving home, of unfulfilling work. Of empty friendships and lacquered alienation. The 12 Step program, which has saved my life, will change the life of anyone who embraces it. I have seen it work many times with people with addiction issues of every hue: drugs, sex, relationships, food, work, smoking, alcohol, technology, pornography, hoarding, gambling, everything. Because the instinct that drives the compulsion is universal. It is an attempt to solve the problem of disconnection, alienation and tepid despair, because the problem is ultimately 'being human' in an environment that is curiously ill-equipped to deal with the challenges that entails. We are all on the addiction scale.

Those of us born with clear-cut and blatant substance addiction are in many ways the lucky ones. We alcoholics and junkies have minimized our mystery to tiny cycles of craving and fulfilment. Our pattern is easier to observe and therefore, with commitment and help, easier to resolve.

If your personal pattern happens to be the addiction equivalent of the 'long form con-trick', as opposed to a 'short grift', it can take ages to know just what your problem is. If you're addicted to bad relationships, bad food, abusive bosses, conflict or pornography, it can take a lifetime to spot the problem, and apparently a lifetime is all we have. This book is not just about extremists like me. No, this is a book about you.

Do you have that sense that something is missing? A feeling in your gut that you're not good enough? That if you tick off some action, whether it's eating a Twix, buying some shoes, smoking a joint or getting a good job, you will feel better? If you do, it's hardly surprising because I believe we live in an age of addiction where addictive thinking has become almost totally immersive. It is the mode of our culture. Consumerism is stimulus and response as a design for life. The very idea that you can somehow make your life alright by attaining primitive material goals – whether it's getting the ideal relationship, the ideal job, a beautiful Berber rug or forty quids' worth of smack – the underlying idea, 'if I could just get X, Y, Z, I would be okay', is consistent and it is quite wrong.

Addiction is when natural biological imperatives, like the need for food, sex, relaxation or status, become prioritized to the point of destructiveness. It is exacerbated by a culture that understandably exploits this mechanic as it's a damn good way to sell Mars bars and Toyotas. In my own blessedly garish addiction each addictive pursuit has been an act of peculiar faith that the action will solve a problem.

In this book we will discuss, with me doing most of the talking, how we can overcome our destructive and oppressive habits, be liberated from tyrannical thinking and move from the invisible inner prison of addiction to a new freedom in the present.

What makes me qualified for such a task? A task which, in a different lexicon, might be called achieving peace, mindfulness, personal fulfilment, or yet more grandly 'enlightenment', 'nirvana' or 'Christ-consciousness'? Certainly not some personal, ethical high ground. My authority comes not from a steep and certain mountain top of po-faced righteousness. This manual for Self-Realization comes not from the mountain but from the mud. Being human is a 'me too' business. We are all in the mud together. My qualification is that I am more addicted, more narcissistic, more driven by lust and the need for power and recognition. Every single pleasure-giving thing that's come my way from the cradle in Grays to the Hollywood chaise longue has been grabbed and guzzled and fondled and fucked and smoked and sucked and for what? Ashes.

Do you sometimes question whether you even have the option or right to be happy? The churning blank march of metropolitan life feels like the droning confirmation that joy is not an option. Escalators like conveyor belts to a mass grave, grey streets like a yard. Thank God, I've not (yet!!) been to prison but when I think about the levels of categorization from worst to least awful, I ponder freedom in general. Worst – being locked alone in a solitary cell in a category A, maximum security prison – to less awful, with increasing tidbits of liberty through categories B and C, with privileges like a kitchen job or a library job (if *The Shawshank Redemption* is to be believed), down to an open prison where inmates can cycle into town for a few hours. How much further along this scale of freedom is the life of a man or woman in a drab flat, imprisoned by drug addiction, surviving on benefits, or anyone trapped in a job they hate, or a kid at

> 'If you're addicted to bad relationships, bad food, abusive bosses, conflict or pornography, it can take a lifetime to spot the problem, and apparently a lifetime is all we have. This book is not just about extremists like me. No, this is a book about you.'

a school they'd rather swerve, all living with twisted and anxious guts? Or my life? Or your life? I'm not saying that it's worse to have a job in London that you hate than to be a jolly C-cat prisoner, skipping off to the workshop twirling a spanner; I'm saying that we are all in prisons of varying categories.

Hang on to your hat and grab your pistol of cynicism in preparation to gun me down here and now, because I'm about to allude to how a recent experience in my mollycoddled life made me feel like I was in a first-class penitentiary. On tour in Australia I was travelling in air-locked privilege from plane to car to delightful hotel room to arena when struck from within by a yearning to escape that I couldn't ignore. I arrived in Brisbane at a towering and chintzy hotel and was taken to a room that blasted me with immaculate comfort but when the door closed behind the perfectly friendly guard and I was alone I couldn't open a window, because, y'know, these buildings are high and it's dangerous. Presumably due to suicide. You cannot get to air, the air you breathe is packaged and one of the few commodities of our wasteful age that is fastidiously recycled.

Now I hope I'm not trying to dress up a tantrum as an epiphany here, but I felt trapped, that I had no way back to nature, nature like the sky, nature like the sky inside, there was no way to breathe, to be a human. Suddenly I felt I had to scramble to have access to natural conditions, in one jarring moment I felt the g-force of the rapid journey from hunter-gatherer to hunted and gathered. No wonder people hanker after animalism and raw thrills. No wonder people go dogging, hot real breath on a windscreen, torch lights and head lights searching, huddled strangers clutching in the dark for the piercing relief of orgasm. No wonder people use porn, hunched over a laptop, grasping and breathless, serious and dutiful like a zealous attendant clerk at a futile task. From this form of escape I am not long exempt. I usually laugh afterwards. As soon as the biological objective has been reached I am ejected from the mindless spell. I look down on myself and sometimes enquire out loud, 'What was that all about?', like some monkey man coming to consciousness, and I glance back transcended, 'Was that honestly your best idea at solving the way you feel? Now get me some tissues and a bible.'

What are we doing when we're masturbating? Or swallowing mindless food? Or swilling silly drinks? Who there do we serve? What is the plan?

The feeling I had in the hotel is real. The need for connection. The feeling I had when I used drugs was real. The feeling, the need, is real. The feeling you have that 'there's something else' is real.

What happens when you don't follow the compulsion? What is on the other side of my need to eat and purge? The only way to find out is to not do it, and that is a novel act of faith.

Incidentally here's how I actually solved the 'problem', I left the hotel at daybreak. I wish I could say I moved into a 'community of indigenous peoples down by the river' where we grew our own veg and sang songs about our ancestors and an elder gave me a tattoo of a rabbit God on my groin and told me I had real spirit and gave me a tribal name, and it was then I knew my purpose – 'to connect with the Great Unknown', to weave the consciousness of man and the consciousness of nature into a perfect tapestry, to tell the story of oneness with such clarity that God Herself would come to the aid of the good and nature would rise through torrents and branches, flames and feathers and flood, and deliver us unto heaven. The still and ever-present heaven within.

But actually I just moved to a better hotel with a balcony.

Nihilism has quietly risen then, a pessimistic acceptance of point-lessness reigns in every addict, pleasure a defibrillator to jerk us along. Now, with fourteen and a half years gratefully drug-free, I identify strongly still when I hear of someone who just can't stay clean. I understand. I remember, more than remember, I occasionally relive. 'I know this won't work, this fix, this drink, this destructive and unlovely act but it will give me distraction from now, for now. And that is enough.'

Here's some good news for the fallen, for those of you that are reading this in despair, the junkies, the alkies, the crack-heads, anorexics, bulimics, dyspeptics, perverts, codependent, love-addicted, hopeless cases: I now believe addiction to be a calling. A blessing. I now hear a rhythm behind the beat, behind the scratching discordant sound of my constant thinking. A true pulse behind the bombastic thud of the ego drum. There, in the silence, the offbeat presence of another thing. What could it be, this other consciousness? Just the sublime accompaniment to my growing nails, pumping heart and rushing blood? These physical and discernible bodily phenomena, do they have a counterpart in a world less obvious? Are we addicts like the animals that evidently pre-emptively fled the oncoming tsunami, sensing some foreboding? Are we attuned to prickling signals that demand anaesthesia? What is the pain? What is it? What does it want?

Now, let's not forget in all the excitement that this is a self-help book, a guide to tackling addiction in all its forms, a guide that will encompass certain principles that, if followed, will free you from the misery, however quiet or consuming, of your condition. An integral, unavoidable and in fact one of the best parts of this process is developing a belief in a Higher Power. Not that you have to become some sort of religious nut. Well actually you already are a religious nut, if you take 'religious nut' to mean that you live your life adhering to a set of beliefs and principles and observances concerning conduct. Most people in the West belong to a popular cult of individualism and materialism where the pursuit of our trivial, petty desires is a daily ritual. If you're reading this specifically because you have addiction issues, whether to substances or behaviours, you are in an advanced sect with highly particular and devotional practices, sometimes so ingrained they don't even have to be explicitly 'thought', they are intensely and unthinkingly believed. 'If I find Miss Right, all will be well.' 'If I can get my rocks off, or yawn down a pint of ice cream, I'll be okay.' What this program asks us to consider is the possibility of hope. Hope that a different perspective is possible. Hope that there is a different way.

To undertake this process, the pursuit of happiness, or contentment or presence or freedom, we have to believe that such a thing is obtainable.

Through this, the rather grim and at times, let's face it, bloody glamorous research of my life I've inadvertently happened upon some incredible people and ideas that, one day at a time, sometimes one moment at a time, lift me out of the glistening filth and into the presence of something ancient and timeless which I believe, no matter what your problem, will give you access to The Solution.

The Twelve Steps

You know me, right? You know I hate systems, especially 'The System', a bogus set of instructions for us, the people, to follow, while the truly free wallow in privilege. So imagine my initial resistance to this system, the 12 Steps, 'Don't tell me what to do, I'm an individual, I'm a maverick, I'm a hustler, I'm a poet wandering through the wind-lashed wilderness screaming my song into the po-faced and judgemental world.'

Especially as, in its original form, the 12 Steps says the word God as freely and as frequently as an ecclesiastical Tourette's sufferer. I sat in chilly rooms in the British countryside all chastened and desperate, looking at these bleak edicts on the wall, thinking, 'maybe for you, but not for me'. Curiously, later examination of these principles revealed that self-centred, egotistical thinking is the defining attribute of the addictive condition. Self-centredness is a tricky thing; it encompasses more than just vanity. It's not just Fonzie, looking at himself in self-satisfied wonder and flexing his little tush, no. Here is a more opaque example of self-centredness. If your partner is a bit wayward, you know selfish or difficult and you cast yourself as the downtrodden carer, pacing behind them going, 'I don't know what they'd do without me', that is another form of self-centredness. You are making yourself and your feelings about the situation the ontological (steady!) centre of the world. Is there a different way that you could be you? Especially as we all know, don't we, the you being you and me being me is the absolute alpha and omega of the world today, flick on a TV, glance at your feed, it's all about me, me, me, the perfect product, holiday, hair tonic, telephone provider for my unique self. Well that's just fine and dandy, but I don't really know what 'me' is or what 'me' wants and now I'm beginning to question if thinking about 'me' all day is doing 'me' any good.

The first time I saw the Steps, I thought, 'Hmm, a bit religious, a bit pious, a bit ambitious'. There was the 'Christiany' feel. Look at the third step, 'turn our will and our lives over to the care of God' – steady on old boy, that just sounds like a cosy version of ISIS.

But now I know that you could be a devout Muslim with a sugar problem, an atheist Jew who watches too much porn, a Hindu who can't stay faithful, or a humanist who shops more than they can afford to and this program will effortlessly form around your flaws and attributes, placing you on the path you were always intended to walk, making you, quite simply, the best version of yourself it is possible to be. In my case, as you will see, this includes a good many flaws, some odd thoughts and occasional behavioural outbursts.

23

If this is your first time looking at the steps, note your own feelings toward them.

1. We admitted that we were powerless over our addiction, that our lives had become unmanageable.

2. We came to believe that a Power greater than ourselves could restore us to sanity.

3. We made a decision to turn our will and our lives over to the care of God *as we understood Him*.

4. We made a searching and fearless moral inventory of ourselves.

5. We admitted to God, to ourselves and to another human being the exact nature of our wrongs.

6. We were entirely ready to have God remove all these defects of character.

7. We humbly asked Him to remove our shortcomings.

8. We made a list of all persons we had harmed, and became willing to make amends to them all.

9. We made direct amends to such people wherever possible, except when to do so would injure them or others.

10. We continued to take personal inventory and when we were wrong promptly admitted it.

11. We sought through prayer and meditation to improve our conscious contact with God *as we understood Him*, praying only for knowledge of His will for us and the power to carry that out.

12. Having had a spiritual awakening as a result of these steps, we tried to carry this message to addicts, and to practise these principles in all our affairs.

Here is how I look at these steps now, and it's how I invite you to look at them too. It certainly demsytifies it. I've probably overcompensated with the 'f' word, but my point is that this is a practical system that anyone can use.

1 Are you a bit fucked?

2 Could you not be fucked?

3 Are you, on your own, going to 'unfuck' yourself?

4 Write down all the things that are fucking you up or have ever fucked you up and don't lie, or leave anything out.

5 Honestly tell someone trustworthy about how fucked you are.

6 Well that's revealed a lot of fucked up patterns. Do you want to stop it? Seriously?

7 Are you willing to live in a new way that's not all about you and your previous, fucked up stuff? You have to.

8 Prepare to apologize to everyone for everything affected by your being so fucked up.

9 Now apologize. Unless that would make things worse.

10 Watch out for fucked up thinking and behaviour and be honest when it happens.

11 Stay connected to your new perspective.

12 Look at life less selfishly, be nice to everyone, help people if you can.

What about my precious individuality though? I can't subject my unique mind to a system, 'the philosophical prison ain't been built that can hold me, baby!' That may well be and resisting authority is all fine and dandy, but the point of that surely is to resist being oppressed or exploited by that authority? There is no oppression or exploitation here. Furthermore, and dim the lights and cue the *Twilight Zone* music, 'Who is the me that I am trying to protect?', that's a question that we'll ponder over these chapters and possibly answer. Although, I'll be honest, the riddle of understanding the true nature of Self has baffled the finest minds humanity has had to offer since time began. Still, I like a challenge.

Now, in the way I had to substitute the word 'addiction' for 'drugs', you might need to make a substitution of your own. For food, tech, gambling, obsessive relationships, porn – in fact whatever it is that you want to change. Think of yourself as a computer with a virus and this as a code that will cleanse you. If you follow this path, if you do the things suggested in this book, it will induce a change in you.

If then you have an obvious addiction issue, you are in luck: there exists already an incredibly effective method for tackling it and redirecting the destructive energy of your condition into a new way of being. You'll find much identification in this book and it'll be a useful companion to the other literature and support groups that are available. If you have a more wily malady, a sadness, a dissatisfaction, a longing that you are dealing with in ineffectual instalments, I promise you that if we earnestly apply this program to your life, your perception will alter and with it, your world.

There are now hundreds of 12 Step movements with new objects of unwitting fetishization: narcotics, gambling, food, gaming, sex, hoarding. There are in fact now sufficient organizations successfully deploying this method for us to assert that there is a common yearning that initiates, then fuels, the addictive cycle. When I first encountered the 12 Steps I had to apply them to drugs and alcohol. They worked. Then sex, food and work. They are working. Now I apply them to every thought or feeling I have, knowing they are a means of negotiating my experience of the external world and my place within it. My professional life, my domestic life, my spiritual life and my new life as a dad are all lived via a map that has been drawn up using these principles. No two people use the 12 Steps in the same way, written into them are multiple clauses that allow for limitlessly diverse individuality.

Where I have found this program most rewarding and yet most challenging is in the way that it has unravelled my unquestioned faith that I was the centre of the universe and that the purpose of my life was to fulfil my drives, or if that wasn't possible, be miserable about it in colourful and creative ways. So whilst this program will work for you regardless of creed or lack of creed, it will also disabuse you of the notion, however conscious of it you are, that you and your drives are the defining motivations for your life. The reason I worked the 12 Steps was because I was desperate. The reason I continue to is because they have awakened me to the impossibility of happiness based on my previous world view: that I am the centre of the world and that what I want is important.

I can attest personally that the 12 Steps work with severe addiction issues. If you have them, you should engage with the appropriate 12 Step support group. My hope for this book is that wherever you are on the scale of addiction, chronically ill or privately concerned or simply seeking change, you will benefit from working these steps in the way I did, honestly, openly and willingly.

If you're like me, you like to 'half-arse' things. Me, I'll buy a book on healthy eating or meditation and that'll be enough, I will use the social tool of 'consumerism' to satiate a need and leave the matter there. A book on healthy eating untouched on the shelf will not improve my Body Mass Index, whatever the hell that is. A book on meditation, flung to one side, will not elevate my consciousness and attune me to the Great Oneness behind my thoughts and feelings. If you're not going to do the things suggested in the book you may as well spend the money on cake or blow it down the track. It also, and I don't really want to tell you this, isn't easy. This isn't 'How to change your life in ten minutes while sat on your arse writing messages to the universe and popping them under your pillow.' It's bloody difficult. It is the hardest thing I've ever done. Actually no, the hardest thing I've ever done is toil under the misapprehension that I could wring pleasure out of the material world, be it through fame, money, drugs or sex, always arriving back at the same glum stoop of weary dissatisfaction.

That's why the first step is saying, 'I'm fucked, it's not improving, I want to change.' Tacitly you have done that by reading this far.

1

Are you a bit fucked?

Step 1: We admitted that we were powerless over our addiction, that our lives had become unmanageable.

This is an invitation to change. This is complicated only in that most of us are quite divided, usually part of us wants to change a negative and punishing behaviour, whereas another part wants to hold on to it. For me Recovery is a journey from a lack of awareness to awareness. Let me tell you what I mean using my own vanilla experience as a bog-standard drug addict and alcoholic.

I always felt I was rather too clever for something like a 'program for living', certainly one that had any religious overtones. It's not that I thought that religion was 'the opiate of the masses', if it was, I would've had some, I loved opium. It's that I thought it was dumb. Drab, dry, dumb, shouty, hysterical, dumb. Small-town dumb. Foreign dumb. Take Christianity, either it's so medieval and swathed in pageantry that it's droning and ridiculous or they try and modernize it and make it cheesy. Bad guitars, jumpers and knowing, sympathetic looks. No. Thank. You.

I had two serendipitous licks: one, I was introduced to the 12 Steps by a seriously committed atheist and two, I was privately desperate. I was broken. I had run out of ideas and juice and was only kept moving by inertia. I'd given up thinking about why I felt sad, or different, or hopeless, I just knew I did, and I left that knowledge parked to one side in my mind, unaddressed, ignored, rotting. Meanwhile I drank and used drugs to keep me upright and functioning, to stop the sadness running over. If you had ever tapped me on the shoulder and said, 'Hey Russell, what's your plan?', I may have reflexively spouted some cock-eyed optimism about 'waiting for my break' or 'this time next year I'll be a somebody' but deep down I knew I had no plan. I ask you now, do you have a plan? You don't have to answer me now, in fact, there's very little point in answering me at all, given that I'm not there (you're now alone, reading this!), but can you, in what ought to be the sanctuary of your mind say to yourself: 'I have a plan. I know where I am going.' My way of coping with the quiet anxiety of uncertainty was to find distractions and pleasures. I was never still. I was seldom reflective. I sustained myself with distraction.

Here is a clinically accepted breakdown of the cycle of addiction. If this model is reflective of the aspect of your life that you'd like to change, it's likely that the 12 Step model will too. Let's see:

A 5-point guide to the cycle of addiction

1 Pain
2 Using an addictive agent, like alcohol, food, sex, work, dependent relationships to soothe and distract
3 Temporary anaesthesia or distraction
4 Consequences
5 Shame and guilt, leading to pain or low self-esteem

And off we go again. I'll tell you how this applies to me and you can mentally keep track with its application to your problem – and don't let yourself off the hook if I seem crazier than you, that's my qualification for writing this book, remember. I was in pain. As long as I can remember, I didn't feel good enough. Now I'm a little older I think, 'What does that mean, good enough?', compared to what, when, where, how? But back then, in my gurgling and nervous childhood and rash and frenetic teens I just felt inadequate, incomplete. Not good enough. And it hurt. I looked out at the world as if from within an aquarium and it felt lonely. I also had no technique for addressing that feeling so I had to invent some. That is number 2 on the 5-point guide. I used an addictive agent and in my earliest incarnation of addictive behaviour I used the innocuous toxin, sugar. Chocolate. Food. I put stuff in my mouth and I felt better, what's wrong with that? Forgive me if I'm patronizing you

> You don't have to not drink for twenty years today. You don't have to give up white bread for all eternity, right now. This "one day at a time" cliché when taken plainly is no less profound than any "be in the moment" Eastern wisdom I've since encountered. Today is all I have.'

here, I want you to understand a few crucial points: I was managing my feelings through external means and the object is not in itself bad. There's no point in demonizing chocolate biscuits, they of themselves are not the problem. They won't of their own volition kick down your front door, shine a flashlight in your face as you sleep, drag you from your bed and jam themselves down your throat. The participation of your consciousness is a prerequisite. For some people a chocolate biscuit is a harmless treat. For some a wee drop of rum or saucy nip of smack is a tonic. The heroin will ferry you to crisis more quickly than a chocolate Penguin biscuit but the key point is the function of this external agent in your life. Number 3 is a temporary numbing, the moment of grateful exhalation and relief, post-biscuit, post-coital, post-gratifying text from the object of your obsession, post-whatever it is you're fixing on. Point 4 is 'consequences', what is the price paid? I used to feel awful as a kid after I'd snaffled my way through a week's worth of biscuits in one absent-minded sitting. I don't think there's a person alive who doesn't reproach themselves momentarily after an orgasm achieved in solitude. And after using drugs, when I was coming to the end of my sojourn into substance misuse was the only time I could countenance quitting. Number 5 is 'pain' and we're back to the start of the cycle.

As Eckhart Tolle says, 'addiction starts with pain and ends with pain.' Here we can see that dissected. As the cycle of addiction goes round it gathers momentum, like an out-of-control carousel, like the spinning

> ‘I was a kid, then I was an addict and by the time the idea of working a program had reached me, which with substances means abstinence and with behaviour and food means structure, I was twenty-seven, a heroin addict and in serious trouble.’

of my nauseous head when drunk. The legal age to drink in the UK is eighteen, by the time I was nineteen medical professionals and the teachers at my college had identified I had a problem and were telling me I needed help. In retrospect, it was evident much earlier, in the way I ate, related to people, thought about myself and my sexuality. I wish I could've identified these patterns, this tendency sooner, so I could've begun to apply the methods outlined in this book. For me though things had to get worse, I had to repeat this pattern for ten years with consequences increasing with each vertiginous whip. I didn't know there was another way. I was a kid, then I was an addict and by the time the idea of working a program had reached me, which with substances means abstinence and with behaviour and food means structure, I was twenty-seven, a heroin addict and in serious trouble.

Step 1 invites us to admit that we are using some external thing, a relationship, a drug or a behaviour as the 'power' that makes our life liveable. It asks if this technique is making our life difficult. By admitting we are 'powerless' over whatever it is, we are saying we need a new power, that this current source of power is more trouble than it's worth.

I have made this admission many times and I make it still each day. It began with the admission that I was powerless over drugs and alcohol, they were the most obvious and troublesome power sources that I was using. The 'unmanageability' here meant the negative consequences in my life were stacking up and importantly, once I start with drink and drugs I don't know when, or if, I will stop. The very act of drinking or using sets me on a course that I am unable to reliably arrest. It is admittedly more subtle when applied to pornography and overeating but it is still clear that I have to structure my thinking around these behaviours and that the structure can't be based on compulsive behaviour.

To return to my point about 'two minds', a divided self, my experience of that was as follows. When I first heard about the program and the idea of abstinence was explained I thought both 'fuck that' and a kind of low resonant thud of acceptance that abstinence would be my path. One of the many paradoxes of the spiritual life I encountered here lies in the trite maxim 'one day at a time', as in 'just try not to drink today', 'try not to eat unhealthily today' and 'try not to act out sexually today'. I knew they meant 'you can't ever drink again', 'no more chocolate. Ever' and 'you are now celibate'. 'Your ballroom days are over baby.' And they do mean that. If you are a serious alcoholic, you cannot drink. If you have food issues you will always need structure around eating. We have to accept it. Where the 'one day at a time' homespun, thanks Nan, wisdom kicks in is with the rather Zen and incontrovertible truth that life is experienced in the present, beyond today your projections of life are conceptual. You don't have to not drink for twenty years today. You don't have to give up white bread for all eternity, right now. And if you do make it through today, and wake up tomorrow, what does it really matter that you didn't act out yesterday? I mean, you're not accumulating tokens for punitive pleasure. This 'one day at a time' cliché when taken plainly is no less profound than any 'be in the moment' Eastern wisdom I've since encountered. Today is all I have.

Now that I'm fourteen and a half years clean, one day at a time, I like to riff on this concept like I'm Charlie Parker or Foucault. When I feel like

I want to act out sexually, I surrender it, I don't act out. Then the next day, or even an hour later I think, 'Imagine I had done that? It would be over now anyway and I'd've detonated my family'.

Step 1 means you can change. It means surveying the landscape of your life, your family relationships, your working life, your sexual behaviour, your eating, your use of your phone, drugs and alcohol, the way you spend money and asking, 'Am I happy with this?' 'Is this how I want to live?' If there is a behaviour or problem that lurches out garishly, some glaringly obvious looming catastrophe that this surveillance reveals, then it is here that you can take Step 1. I am 'powerless over this and my life has become unmanageable.'

This unmanageability concept is interesting too and as well as the more obvious interpretation of chaos and disorder there is a deeper, scarier meaning. The first aspect in my case was plainly observable: unpaid debts, hospital visits, jobs lost, relationships lost, friends holding up their hands and reversing out of my life. I was creating chaos. I had followed another well-known 12 Step trope, 'First my using was fun, then fun with problems, then just problems.' The positive aspects of my character were becoming redundant, it didn't matter that I was bright, or kind or talented, these traits were being diluted to the point of irrelevance by the seeping negativity of my addiction. The unmanageability though has a disturbing and, in my case, demonstrable clause: when I yield control to that part of myself, when I drink or use or say 'fuck it' around any destructive behaviour, I don't know when I'll get my life back or what state it will be in when I do. The unmanageability at its heart means that there is a beast in me. It is in me still. I live in negotiation with a shadow side that has to be respected. There is a wound. I believe that this is more than a characteristic of addiction. I think it is a part of being human, to carry a wound, a flaw and again, paradoxically, it is only by accepting it that we can progress.

I took Step 1 when I 'admitted I was powerless over my addiction and that my life had become unmanageable.' That I didn't have control, no matter what I said to myself and others, and that it was getting worse. I knew there was no way out, that I had fear and shame that I didn't want to face, that I hoped I would never have to. That I would be able, through my will, to bend the world into making me feel alright somehow.

When I met Chip Somers, bloody ridiculous name, I know, who ran the treatment centre where I got clean, he was the first 12 Step person I spoke to. He never mentioned 'God' or 'Higher Power', as I say he's a hardcore atheist, he makes Richard Dawkins look like Uri Geller, he just told me straight, 'You are fucked. If you carry on using like you are, in six months' time you'll be in prison, a lunatic asylum or a grave.' And whilst I was a little shocked, I knew he was right.

You might not be addicted to crack and heroin as I was and the above might seem comfortingly alien so I should tell you, I've since worked Step 1 many times. With food, I am powerless over food; if I start eating chocolate, I don't know when I'll stop. With sex, if I make sex the panacea, the salve to this pain we discussed earlier, I will soon lose control of my sexual conduct and I'll end up in more pain. Or work. Or my relationship. In fact I now work this program and therefore this step in a 360-degree fashion. I have no power at all over people, places and things, and if I ever for a moment mistakenly believe that I do – and act as if I do – pain is on its way. If there is something in your life that is causing you a problem and you're aware of it, I bet you've tried using will, crystals, hypnotism and pills to placate it. My suspicion is they haven't worked and my experience is they never will. Oddly, counterintuitively, in our culture of individualism and self-centred valour, it is by surrendering that we can begin to succeed. It is by 'admitting that we have no power' that we can begin the process of accessing all the power we will ever need. I've heard it said that we have the '-ism' before we have the addiction. I now attest to the presence of a conflagratory condition that awaits the substance to ignite it. Now with fourteen and a half years drug- and alcohol-free I cannot clearly say whether it was in sex or drugs that my addiction found its truest expression. Certainly drugs and alcohol have the power to decimate your life with greater efficiency. But my escalation through so-called recreational drugs to hard drugs was underscored by a uniform pain. Many of the associated problems that addiction evokes are caused by their criminal status and poverty. What doesn't change, regardless of the manner in which addiction is materialized or the economic conditions of the afflicted, is the presence of pain.

Pain is a signal, it's some aspect of us that's beyond our somewhat narrow conception of 'self', communicating. A pain in the leg means 'don't put pressure on this leg'; a pain in the mind means 'change the way you live'. With earlier manifestations of the same condition the signals were not easy to read.

The impulse that made me eat too much chocolate when I was a kid was the same impulse that led me to heroin addiction in a child-friendly, socially acceptable disguise. Or when I was watching too much TV, even then as a little boy, I was using external resources to medicate because I felt uneasy inside. My personal circumstances may have contributed to this, my mum was ill a lot and I had a tense relationship with my stepdad, but these biographical details are less important than the sense I had that something was missing.

When I was a kid, knelt in front of the TV in the post-school, pre-Mum-home hinterland, I believed I had a solution to the problem of being me with every Penguin biscuit I jammed into my gawping trap. The distraction of the taste, the ritual of unpeeling them like a Buffalo Bill victim, the scraping of the chalk-brown custard guts, enough to occupy me, to fill me up. So the 'treat' of a perfectly

> For me, today, on this planet I thankfully aspire to more than brief interludes of numbness through food, sex and the acquisition of delightful tight trousers with unpronounceable names; particularly as I now know they are all ciphers, poor facsimiles of the thing I'm actually seeking.'

enjoyable chocolate biscuit sandwich-wrapped in foil became an emotional necessity, a survival tool. Alone at home they toppled like a row of calorific dominoes into the hungry void. I already had a sense of shame and solitude around this behaviour. There was already something other than the simple eating of biscuits at play.

When through the storm of puberty I graduated to porn, in those charming sepia, stuck-together pages of yesteryear, it was – I know now – the same impulse that led me to the chapel of the lavvy for masturbatory distraction and temporary connection and relief.

God help the trainee perverts of today as they stand Kleenex in hand on the brink of a Niagara of every conceivable kink, accessible with any smart device they can cram into their clammy palms. Porn is a clear example of how our culture is feeding the disease of addiction. The natural impulse to have sex becomes a compulsion to masturbate. The attraction to connect is culturally translated by pornography into a numb and lonely staring strum at broken digital ghosts. The most physically creative thing we have, reduced to a dumb shuffle that'd embarrass a monkey.

Of course if you'd told me at fourteen that we were a decade away from a porn paradise I would've toppled back in Damascene spasms at the prospect and scoffed at any pious talk of it being corrosive.

Because I had no code for life, no awareness that what I was doing was problematic. In fact porn, such as it was then, hedge-snatched, stained and shared rags, was the solution I'd discovered to the problem of being me. And it is a strong medicine.

I'm writing this on a laptop and I'm forty-one years old and the temptation to look at porn is still there. So how am I, in this moment, the moment which all enlightened folk agree is the only moment we actually have, going to avoid looking at porn? Here is the process. I recognize that I have looked at porn before and I know what the results were then. It was distracting and numbing, which is good, but it didn't provide any real comfort – if I'm honest I felt a bit worse. The 12 Steps along with the support of others who understand how I think and feel, whether that's the trivial urge to use porn or suicidal thoughts are the only method I know of for disrupting detrimental habits.

As a side note it's worth mentioning that this is not a moral argument, for example if you love looking at porn and don't have a problem with it, then I have no opinion on that or advice to offer. In fact, if you're happy with your wanking or boozing or drug use, or self-esteem or relationships or eating, you probably don't need this book. If there's not a problem, there's not a problem, as they say in 12 Step organizations. For me, today, on this planet I thankfully aspire to more than brief interludes of numbness through food, sex and the acquisition of delightful tight trousers with unpronounceable names; particularly as I now know they are all ciphers, poor facsimiles of the thing I'm actually seeking.

I know, then, that looking at porn won't make me feel any better. That to look at porn, even though I have this knowledge, would be a pointless re-tread of a well-worn path. But, as with heroin, chocolate bars or relationships with inappropriate partners, knowing it won't work has not stopped me indulging. As if I have a negative faith in a self-destructive doctrine that life cannot be better than it is now, that I don't deserve better, that I am worthless and dirty so who cares what I do to cope?

Once I topple, go active, decide to pursue my nominated object of addiction, I inwardly switch to a circuit of behaviour that is distinct from my better nature. The Jekyll and Hyde story is an apposite allegory and most addicts identify with the radical transition that occurs once they are triggered. There's no point you (in this instance in the role of a Victorian flower girl) pleading with Mr Hyde not to ravage you and kick over your begonias, telling him that he will 'regret it in the morning' because Mr Hyde doesn't give a fuck on a stick. Far safer to ask Dr Jekyll to stop messing around with alchemy, when he is clearly dangerously unqualified, before he's taken that first drink. I don't know what he got his doctorate in. I bet it's one of those ones where the university just gave him a mortarboard and cape for turning up and giving a lecture.

Once I go, I've gone. There have been many instances in my life where in the midst of some self-generated chaos I've been granted the benefit of hindsight whilst the event is still unfolding. It often takes the form of a mental bird's-eye view, I seem to float up out of me, a yard or two above the carnage I've created and look down at other me thinking, 'Oh look, there I am, I'm actually persevering with this mayhem. It's almost certainly a terrible idea. Oh well too late now, I might as well jump back in with him and finish this shit off.' This is not diminished responsibility; I am responsible for all the things I've done. It's just I wasn't *this* me while I was doing them.

My life is about preserving the conditions where it is less likely that I will quantum leap into the other guy.

To overcome that troubling and cyclical mentality, I had to believe that my life could be better. Whether that's better than a life as a drug addict fourteen years ago, or better now today by not looking at pornography. The consequences of my addiction were more palpable and severe when I was using drugs. The pace of deterioration too was, in retrospect, worrying. Most days were tarnished with a volatile emotional episode, physical injury, conflict, arrest, humiliation or violence. I was very fortunate and will remain forever grateful that people intervened in my enthusiastic rush to the gutter. In this book you will read much that might make you think, 'I'm not as bad as him', or, 'he's still a nutter', but the transformation I have experienced as the result of these steps is the important thing and is cause for great hope in anyone suffering from addiction. This idea of hope we shall explore in the next chapter. For now let's summarize what we've discussed.

- Do you have a problem? Is there some activity – drinking, eating, spending money, gambling, watching porn, destructive relationships, promiscuity, in fact any behaviour that is impairing your ability to enjoy life (and life can be enjoyable), that you are engaging in and are struggling to stop?

- If the answer is no, well done, carry on, you should have plenty of time on your hands to help others less fortunate and generally serve the planet and its people.

- If you're not sure, take a moment. Sit quietly in a place where you won't be disturbed. Close your eyes. Move your attention to your breathing, the rhythm of the breath; each inhalation a new beginning, each exhalation a new ending. Do you feel anxious? Afraid? Disturbed? Is your mind constantly shuffling through thoughts, restless? Is it difficult to sit and do nothing? Do you ever do this or are you, as I was for many years, constantly involved in activity or distraction? What happens when you sit alone with your breath, your breath that will one day cease? For me it usually begins as an uneasy experience, even now after years of meditation (and by now I'm sure you'll have spotted that I'm trying to trick you into meditating). I have to practise stillness to be comfortable with it, to be comfortable being 'born again' in each new moment. To see that there is no way into the kingdom of heaven except through 'I', through Self, through the experience of thought, feeling, action. The constant witness. A common meditation is to envisage the moment before death, to accept that this place of consciousness in which we sit, that which we call 'I', is the place from which we will experience death. In your mind gently, without pushing, repeat a word that comes to you. It could be 'flower' or 'peace' or 'West Ham' – ideally a word that you associate with serenity or nothing at all. I mean it won't be helpful to sit there inwardly repeating the word 'Hitler' or 'Fuck off' – it's the wrong attitude. Be comfortable. Be relaxed. Release the tension from your face and shoulders and after a while ask yourself, the inner voice, the part of you that has always been there, when you were a kid, when your heart was broken, every time you've ever felt unloved, alone or lost, this voice, this continuing perspective that is in fact the thing that lets you know that you are you and not just some bundle of organs and limbs, the thing with which your memories are threaded together, the bulb which shines your aspirations onto the screen of knowing. Ask this thing, 'Am I serving you?' 'Am I happy?' 'Do I have a problem?'

If the answer is yes, then proceed.

Before You Start: You are going to like working this program a lot. I'll tell you why. It is made for you by you, using a formula that will not exclude or undermine any of your current beliefs.

Step 1 Exercises: Are you a bit fucked?

Here are some questions to ask yourself. They are a good way of getting clarity around your condition, addiction, call it what you will. Hey, it's only language man!

- **What do I want to change?** *Is it drinking? Is it being unable to put my phone down for an hour? Is it self-harm? Is it going out with inappropriate men? Is it thinking negative thoughts about myself? Is it lying? Heroin? Come on, how many examples do you need? I can't do this for you, you know!*
- **What pain or fear do I associate with change in this area?** *I won't fit in? There'll be no joy in life? I won't cope without it? People won't like me? What is it?!*
- **What pleasure am I getting out of not changing?** *Cakes are delicious? Cutting myself relieves me? This activity takes me out of myself?*
- **What will it cost me if this doesn't change?** *My husband will leave? I'll go to prison? I'll get fat? I'll continue to be miserable?*
- **What are the benefits I could gain by having this changed?** *My relationship/health/work will improve?*
- **How has this problem placed my important relationships in jeopardy?** *Friends don't wanna know me? My girlfriend feels used/not respected?*
- **Have I lost respect/reputation due to this problem?** *Come on, do you still need the examples?*

- Has this problem made my home life unhappy? *This is obvious! You can do this yourself.*
- Has this problem caused any type of illness? *Again, just use common sense.*
- Do I turn to the type of person that enables me to practise this behaviour or to companions who enable me? *These questions really get under the skin, huh?*
- What part of the problem do the people who care about me object to most?
- What type of abuse has happened to me and others due to this problem? *Have I neglected my kids? Nagged my husband too much? Or slept with someone I shouldn't have?*
- What have I done in the past to try to fix, control or change this area of my life? *Diets? Setting targets? Moving house? Buying a new hat?*
- What are the feelings, emotions and conditions I have tried to alter or control with this problem? *Sadness? Loneliness? Fear? Work worries? Unhappiness with partner?*
- Right now, if this is such an important area in my life, why haven't I changed?
- Am I willing to do whatever it takes to have this changed, healed or transformed?

If the answer is yes, then write out, go on, get a pen and paper (what do you mean you're on the train, reading this on your phone? Stop making excuses) and write out:

'I admit I am powerless over (whatever you are working the steps on) *and that my life in this area is unmanageable. I cannot, on my own, with my present understanding, consistently manage this problem.'*

2

Could you not be fucked?

Step 2: We came to believe that a Power greater than ourselves could restore us to sanity.

This step is about hope. We've just admitted we have a problem and that our lives have become unmanageable. It's normal to expect that this kind of admission will come as a blow to the ego. It is our ego who up until now has been running the show, with a bit of help from whatever behaviour or substance we've just been forced to accept is a problem.

After I admitted I had a problem I felt weak and pathetic. I felt cracked. Even thinking about not using drugs made me feel hopeless. This is because drugs gave me comfort and the power I needed to survive. Before I stopped taking them, even admitting that my drug-taking was a problem heightened my despair. So we need hope: hope that we can change, hope that there is another way. I can tell you plainly that there is. I can tell you this from lived experience and from what I've observed in others. You might think you are not as bad an addict as I was. I've seen people use this program to overcome addictions that were less outwardly severe, addictions to marijuana, sex, food or binge drinking. You might think that your addiction is much worse than mine. Well I know thousands of people who make my drug use look as wayward as a copper dancing with a woman in a bikini at Notting Hill Carnival. Chip Somers, who if you met him now you might think had spent his whole life playing dominoes in a library, was a right jailbird smack-head, bank-robbing social liability. Nowadays he won't drink caffeine. In whatever area you are struggling I can trot out some example of a beaming do-gooder who has turned their life around using this program. From socially acceptable problems like smoking and crap relationships to stories of depravity that make *Trainspotting* seem aspirational. The stories and the using are infinitely variable, the feelings behind them consistent and the program that provides a way out reliably universal. There is good reason for you to have hope.

You've faced obstacles, inner and outer, that have prevented you from becoming the person you were "meant to be" and that is what we are going to recover.'

Not just cross yer fingers, 'cosmic ordering' type hope either. Reasoned and empirical hope, based on the experience of others who have followed the program that's outlined here.

There will be action, there will be analysis, there will be work, catharsis, sacrifice and suffering. Change is hard, that's why we can't do it alone and why it is vital that we have a foundation of hope. You needn't immediately assume the idiotic and unfounded optimism of a radio breakfast DJ. You need only allow gentle hope to enter your heart. Exhale and allow hope, and give yourself some time. This is a process of change that requires a good deal of self-compassion, which is neither stagnant nor permissive. We can just start by being a little kinder to ourselves and open to the possibility that life doesn't have to be bloody awful.

The feeling of hopelessness is often the first thing revealed when the primary addictive behaviour is challenged or arrested. The reason I was taking drugs was because I felt hopeless. It was the best idea I could come up with to tackle it.

A 'Power greater than ourselves' is a phrase that gets unduly complicated. Like a lot of people with addiction issues, I pick away at concepts, ruminating and nervously reflecting. Are we alone in the universe? What are the forces that drive nature? What initiated this process? Did anything initiate this process? Is time even real? What the hell is consciousness anyway? It isn't helpful, necessary or relevant to wander off into an epistemological labyrinth at this formative stage of recovery. In practical terms, power is the ability to effect change. On our own we didn't have enough power to change so we need access to a power that exceeds that.

In Step 1 we admitted we were 'powerless' over our addiction, our addiction therefore has power over us. It isn't a tie, a power stalemate: the addiction is the dominant power. My own addiction governed my choices for most of my life. It seemed as if there was no way that pattern would ever change. And yet it did, obviously, so you can take some comfort and hope from that.

But it didn't seem obvious on the 12th of December 2002. It seemed hopeless. If you had seen me then, you wouldn't have said, 'Obviously this guy is going to be fine, he looks about twenty-four hours away from discovering a Power greater than himself'. You would have concluded, correctly, that I was a right mess.

I had been using all day. I had been to Bartok, a bar on Chalk Farm Road, Camden, London and picked up 'two of each' from my 'mate' Gritty. I had used in the toilet and had decided to 'make my rounds' before I went into treatment at Focus, a 12 Step treatment centre for drug addicts and alcoholics. I was very much the kind of person who needed a thorough Step 1. I was sick and frightened, I couldn't stop using, my life was falling apart and getting worse each day, and I couldn't see a way out.

Now whatever power I had then, it was insufficient to move me from using, to not using. I came to believe that 'a Power greater than myself' could restore me to sanity, and it did. It moved me from there, to here. This power comprises the following: I surrendered. I applied these steps to my thinking and acting. I sought the help of others. I helped others. I developed a new perspective.

It doesn't seem like it should work when you look at it on paper, or on your device:

Admit there is a problem, have hope that your life can improve.

So far, that is all that is being asked of you. Being 'restored to sanity' we can take to mean that within us there is a version of ourselves waiting to be realized. A better version. All the while I was rattling around on my picaresque excursion, causing damage inside and outside, there was another version of me waiting to be realized. We are, after all, an organic entity, like a tree, with a code stored in our embryonic form that is set to grow to completion. A tree doesn't face the kind of obstacles a highly socialized mammal does, it might get chopped down, or aggressively pruned or have some wire wrapped round it, but no one is going to say it's too fat or that it'll never amount to anything. But in your life you've faced obstacles, inner and outer, that have prevented you from becoming the person you were 'meant to be' or 'are capable of being' and that is what we are going to recover. That's why we call this process Recovery; we recover the 'you' that you were meant to be.

I use Step 2 still, whenever I am in doubt, whenever I need hope: 'I come to believe a Power greater than myself will restore me to sanity.' In this moment now, in the Lake District, with my girlfriend a new mum, momentarily blue and shattered, home from a trip to the Coniston shops, teary with our daughter in her arms, I am presented with a chance to work my program. When there is a problem, my life could become unmanageable. If I for example say, 'Listen I've got to write, you look after yourself', I know that sounds mental but it's the sort of thing I am capable of saying. Those are the kind of selfish impulses I have. Instead, when that impulse comes up, I quickly assess my role in the situation: 'boyfriend', 'father' – does that guy say 'I'm busy' or is that more the kind of lyric that would be spat from the gob of the Camden Kid circa 2002?

> 'You too, you may think, "yes, I am an addict, I will change the way I drink or eat or think or relate to sexual partners", but surely the craving will find a new expression, like a magnetic field ordering iron filings. You can replace the filings but the pull stays the same.'

I accept there is a problem: my girlfriend needs time to herself. 'I come to believe that a Power greater than myself can restore me to sanity'; it does, the program – which is a power greater than me and my previous way of thinking – tells me in this moment, the only moment I have, to immediately surrender my old idea (in this case the old idea is not 'I must take heroin to be happy', it is 'I am here to write'). The idea is surrendered. The power is the program, the sanity is I recover my role as a good father and boyfriend. And I feel good. I feel good typing on this bed with (quite cool actually) lullabies playing on my phone, my daughter gurgling and cooing contentedly by my side, now that is a miracle, with my girlfriend asleep. Can you see how this could very easily have become a different scenario? I bloody can. Old Russell would not have been able to step outside of his selfishness, he would not have had hope that there could be another way and he didn't really know that sanity existed.

Perhaps you may feel, unless you are yourself a celebrity, that the plausibility of these claims is challenged by my position as a famous person in a celebrity-worshipping world. 'Of course you're alright Russell, you're a celebrity, you've a nice house and access to the best restaurants.' May I tell you that fame, like all the other shimmering sedatives I have sought, is limited in its effectiveness. When the baby starts crying as she just did (I knew I spoke too soon!) or I wake up in the night anxious, or when I am haunted by my fear of death and failure, fame is of little use. No one is famous when they're on the toilet. Except I suppose Elvis.

To be clear, having been poor and now not being poor, I am in no rush to sprint down to Kentish Town dole office bellowing, 'It's me again! Can I have my pittance and desperation back?' I say only this. I am famous and I know a lot of famous people and some of them are among the most discontent and lost people I have ever met. Boo hoo? Yes, boo hoo, but do acknowledge that nothing works as a salve for the pain that for simplicity's sake we shall call addiction. I bet from the swampy seat of your own self-pity you would assume that Prince was having a whale of a time, or that George Michael was 'lovin it'. I think it safe to assume, now, that they were not. They had got to the other side of their dream and discovered, as with all illusions, there was nothing of substance there. Either an artist makes friends with the emptiness of 'success', 'fame', 'glamour', or as we have seen, time and time again, they check out in drab splendour, candles at the end of long driveways, vigils held, questions asked.

Here is a postcard from the other side: fame, luxury items and glamour are not real and cannot solve you, whether it's a pair of shoes, a stream of orgies, a movie career or global adulation. They are just passing clouds of imaginary pleasure. When my girlfriend needs me to act like a grown-up, I don't think, 'thank God I'm famous', I refer to my program. It is much more spectacular and surprising that I became capable of being a good boyfriend and father than it is that I, a denizen of creepy-crawly crack dens, escaped to become a famous comedian.

When I became disillusioned with fame and money it was no different from becoming disillusioned with drugs and alcohol. I tried first of all to get over it with gaudy philanthropy and combative proclamations, using my profile as an expression of dissatisfaction.

Then, slowly as usual, I worked my program. That's how you get from being poor, to being famous, to mouthing off about the System, to writing a book about how disconnected people can connect. By having a program. My tendency, my addiction, will always reassert; that's what a tendency is.

When you do Step 4, you will see how the same patterns and beliefs have governed your life, returning you again and again to the same despair. Every time I am prised free of a painful habit, my morphing condition shifts like mercury into a new behaviour. I can admit to you now that my work in Hollywood was driven by the belief that if I could get 'enough fame', I would be alright. I couldn't get enough, there is not enough. I began commenting on social issues in *The Trews*, thinking, 'I can be of use here. I can use my voice and humour to highlight hypocrisy and exploitation.' But at some indiscernible point I became excited by the power. See, the power again! The power! The idea that something can make me feel good! The ego's love of self-centred power. I can be helping a group of working-class activists retain their homes, saved from the clutches of corporate greed and at some point I'll get turned on by how me and my ego can 'own' it. My best efforts, my best intentions will be sucked into the quagmire if I am not vigilant. You too, you may think, 'yes, I am an addict, I will change the way I drink or eat or think or relate to sexual partners', but surely the craving will find a new expression, like a magnetic field ordering iron filings. You can replace the filings but the pull stays the same. It is only by finding a more powerful magnetic pull that you can change the patterns completely. This can be the program itself, sedulously applied. It can be a support group, made up of like-minded people. It can be an orthodox or traditional idea of God. It can be nature. It can be a unified field of consciousness that supports all phenomena. It frankly doesn't matter and it is entirely for you to choose, as long as it is loving, caring and more powerful than you.

Step 2 Exercises: Could you not be fucked?

- **Do I believe that I need to change?** *Yes. Look at Step 1: I really need to change. My life is unacceptable. My relationships are not working. I am not happy.*

- **Do I accept that change means I must think/feel/act differently?** *Of course, otherwise I'd be the same or just making a gesture.*

- **Do I know people who have made comparable changes that seem quite radical?** *Yes. I know that Russell and millions of other people, some with more serious problems than me, some with less serious problems than me, have used these techniques to change their lives.*

- **Is this change likely to be easy and driven by the ideas I already have, techniques I already use and support systems that I already have access to?** *No. This change is going to mean all of those things will alter and that is scary but I know, at least I believe, that it is possible. It has worked for people in worse situations than me, it will work for me too.*

- **What is my conception of a Power greater than me? Is it nature? Is it consciousness beyond the individual? Is it the power of people coming together in the pursuit of a noble goal? Describe your personal understanding of a power greater than yourself.** *I believe that the mystery of creation and the laws of the universe hold great power in them. I believe that the innate love that human beings have for one another is a power. I believe people's willingness to suffer for a cause is a power. I believe the healing of an injury is a power. Muhammad Ali's sacrifice for what he believed in is a power. The music of Mozart (or Moz), the Sistine Chapel ceiling, George Best – all these allude to some Power that is greater than me. The chances that I have had in life, the people that have loved me and been there for me. There are many examples of a Power greater than myself, alone, with my addiction and my thoughts.*

- **Do I have doubt and prejudice about spirituality and the power of a new perspective to solve my problem? What are**

those doubts and prejudices? *Yes. Sometimes I feel there is so much suffering, in my own life and the lives of others, that there cannot be a Supreme Truth or Divine Connectedness that supersedes all else.*

Mantra

'Limitless consciousness, source of all light and love, please lay aside for me doubt and prejudice and give me willingness to believe that you can solve this problem, too, the way you have solved other problems.'

- **What is my conception of a personal Higher Power? Describe it here.** *I feel that when I meditate I connect to a creative and loving energy that is present in all life. They say all the energy that has ever been is still here now and will always be here. That means there is a totality and I am part of it. When I have an opinion on suffering, it is only that, an opinion. I do not and cannot understand the full context of events that occur in an infinite and eternal universe. It's as if within my finite lifetime I glimpse a second of a three-hour movie and try to understand the entire plot.*
  All I must do is engage with this idea: I will become open to the idea that my conceptions, beliefs and experiences are limited. I will become open to new beliefs and new possibilities. I will become open to the idea that I can live a better, more loving and useful life, even if I don't fully understand how I will do it or what it will be like.
- **Can I now accept there is a power greater than me at work in this cosmos?** *I don't have to ally with it yet, all I have to do is accept that my thoughts and I are not the apex of human experience. Of course I can, it's obvious. In nature and in human affairs, it is obvious there are more powerful forces than me.*
- **Do I know people who have changed their lives and live according to spiritual principles who are connected, happy and real?** *Yes, I know a lot of people who live 12 Step lives who have come a long way and live meaningfully and purposefully and lovingly.*
- **Is this how I'd like to be?** *Yes.*

- Do I know people who have engaged with a new Power and used these techniques to induce revolutionary change in their way of living and thinking and have found a new peace and direction?
- Is this what I want?
- To reiterate, is this how my life is now? Or am I struggling with relationships? My emotions?
- Do I lack purpose and drive?
- Am I creating conflict and chaos?
- Even beyond my primary addictive behaviour (drink/drugs/food/sex/spending/technology) are things hard?
- Am I getting depressed?
- Am I afraid?
- Am I helping others?
- In other areas of my life have I exhibited behaviours that if repurposed could serve me now? Like for example my belief that I can make myself feel better with drugs or sex or tech or the right relationship or job or some chocolate?
- Have I kind of worshipped drugs or my phone or sex or shopping?
- Can I see that this impulse applied to something less mundane, materialistic and shallow may motivate change?
- In fact this problem I have could be seen as the misdirection of a positive impulse if I look at it differently, couldn't it?
- Can I connect to this love within me that I sometimes misdirect?
- Can I connect to the love outside of me that I see in others?
- Can I connect to this Power that I see elsewhere in my life?

Mantra (put this into your own words)

'Divine Power, Supreme Truth, love within and without, guide me to a new way of being. Help me to put aside all previous thoughts and prejudices that I may be open to a "New Way". I ask the creative power deep within me to guide me towards the person I was always meant to be, to seek out relationships and experiences that will move me closer to this Truth.'

3

Are you, on your own, going to 'unfuck' yourself?

Step 3: We made a decision to turn our will and our lives over to the care of God *as we understood Him.*

I did this step with help from an atheist and at the point I took it, I would probably have said I was an atheist too. The step, stripped of reference to divine power, becomes 'You don't know what you're doing – you'd better make a decision to accept help.' This is a big stumbling block for many addicts.

To flash forward to the present day, or to stay where you already are if you're not a time traveller, I am now on Step 12, part of which is to help others. So I spend a significant amount of time around addicts at various stages of recovery. When I encounter addicts that are still using, it is fascinating to observe which of the first three steps will be the obstacle that prevents them realizing change. If it's Step 1, that means they flatly deny they have a problem, 'There's nothing wrong with me', they say, 'I like drinking in the daytime', or, 'Cocaine keeps me thin'. Honestly, they say mad stuff like that. There's not much you can do in these cases except admire the battlements of the fortress of self-imposed unawareness.

When Step 2 is the obstacle, they know they have a problem and admit it but cannot 'come to believe' that there is a better way. They say things like, 'I need to drink, it's the only thing that keeps me sane', or, 'I can't imagine life without drugs'. When confronted with this I can only share with them my own story, identify with their lack of hope but tell them in my experience change is possible, that my current life is proof of that possibility.

When people are resistant to Step 3, it means they accept they have a problem, they believe change *is* possible but they think that they will author that change through self-will, determination, guts, moxy, cunning; whatever it is, they will do it themselves. They will say things like, 'I know I can do this', or, 'I can beat this thing', or, 'I've got this far on me own, I'm gonna keep going'. In such cases I point out that all these attributes upon which they are planning to depend have been long present and of little use so far.

I struggled with each step and took them like a vet-bound dog. In fact when I first saw them written down, I ignored them successfully and took giant leaps in the contrary direction, which was of course, downwards. I was afraid of change. For better or worse I had devised a strategy for survival, a means of coping with my feelings and I was terrified of what I might find if I relinquished it.

A counsellor at the treatment centre where I got clean, herself a woman in recovery, surprised me when she said, 'How clever of you to find drugs. Well done, you found a way to keep yourself alive.' This made me feel quite tearful. I suppose because this woman, Jackie, didn't judge me or tell me I was stupid or tub-thumpingly declare that 'drugs kill'. No she told me I'd done well by finding something that made being me bearable. Addicts talking to one another are apt to find such means of connection. To be acknowledged as a person who was in pain and fighting to survive in my own muddled-up and misguided way made me feel optimistic and understood. It is an example of the compassion addicts need from one another in order to change. Thinking about it, that time, early recovery was lit up by moments of connection such as this. Addiction is a lonely business in whatever form it's suffered. A paralysing loop of unseen, hypnotic, negative thinking and destructive and harmful behaviour. The momentum prevents you from getting off the carousel. Crisis is almost a blessing providing cessation of a kind, and with it, the opportunity for change.

On New Year's Eve 2002 with seventeen days clean I stood in an itchy suit outside a drink-and-drug-free event at some kind of civic centre in Guildford, Surrey. It was dark outside and inside it was much too bright, lit by the beaming smiles that only drink-and-drug-free people can produce. Beaming, clean, gleaming, 'everything's gonna be alright' smiles, like the three little birds by Bob Marley's doorstep.

This was not my prognosis. Everything was not going to be alright. Everything was going to carry on being fucking shit. This night itself could be flung on the pile of evidence that stretched like the Tower of Babel into the empty heavens and offended no one but me. Exhibit A squared to the power of 10: this night, this drinkless, sexless, funless, hopeless night is further proof that I do not belong here, that life is not fun, that there is nothing to aspire to or dream about. Joy is a distraction and drink and drugs are the best solution I can think of to cope with the way this feels.

I was twenty-seven, of course, and running on a painful program of self-destruction. I turned to Lucy, who'd thankfully followed me out of the leisure centre where this social catastrophe was happening, and with what I hoped was incredible poignancy and gravitas said, 'It's not for me all this, Lucy, this "yes we can", "just say no" bullshit. This is not my future. We won't look back on this and say, "Russell used to be a drug addict but through the help of others, belief in a Higher Power and a commitment to being of service he turned his life around". I like drugs, I like drinking, I don't like these people and I don't want to be like them. My story is that I'm an addict, I'm going to stay an addict and I'll be dead in my twenties.'

I meant it, ornamented though it was by the narcissism and self-pity that governed me then, it was wrought with twisted sincerity. Yet, by some power beyond me, I have not used since that day. That cannot be due to self-will or good fortune because I had both of those the entire time. It has come from a change in consciousness induced by a new ideology.

This ideology will help anyone who is prepared to accept it. I found that quite hard. I don't trust people and I don't trust institutions. I don't like being told what to do and I don't like the idea that I'm not in charge of my own destiny. I came to see life differently because other people were kind to me, supportive to me and showed me another way. This doesn't mean that today I'm typing this from a Himalayan laptop, using rays of conscious kinetic energy that I radiate from my eyes. I still struggle. But the system I'm outlining is like having another channel installed in my mind. I can still flick the switch back to Sky News or Babestation, but I know there is a different frequency of being which I can experience and when I do I am kinder and more loving and I feel better being alive. I also do not need to drink and take drugs to cope.

Ideally the first three steps can be worked in the time it takes to nod your head three times: yes I have a problem, yes I see it could improve, yes I see that I will need help and I will accept that help. When someone is in that frame of mind they have a chance. This is the state that you need to achieve to recover.

As the step in its original form says, 'we made a decision' – this is because it is understood that there will likely be prevarication and procrastination. Making a decision to 'turn your life and your will over' means you have acknowledged that your previous attempts to run your own life have failed. That you have had to resort to addictive behaviour to cope and now you cannot stop on your own steam. In making a decision we are conceding mentally and, hopefully, spiritually that we cannot do this alone anymore. That for me was the beginning of humility. To say 'I need help' is not an easy thing for many people, we'd prefer to manipulate people into meeting our needs or struggle along without them. Step 3 has profound and ongoing philosophical merit: I am now continually asking for help. Like most of these steps, their practice begins in crisis but continues

> My life in active addiction was an unexamined matrix of disturbances held at bay by addictive behaviour. The stimulus–response relationship between me, myself and the world was like this: "I'm lonely – have sex", "I'm sad – get drunk", "I'm bored – eat a cake". It probably wasn't even that articulate.'

in everyday living. For me making a decision to 'hand over my life and my will' is a daily practice.

Each morning as my habitual negative pattern of mental self-damnation fires up, I interject mentally with my intent to hand my day over. Somebody once said, 'What does that mean, *handing my life and will over to God*? I might as well put it in the microwave', which I thought was pretty funny, because the idea of bundling up your life and will into a ball and kicking it into a benevolent ether doesn't sound like an intelligent way to tackle despair. Step 3 means we ask for help. When I notice that I am agitated, fearful or confused, I no longer, as in the past, plough on. I pause. I have learned to better commune with my feelings. Mentally the inner dialogue is like this: 'Wow. That is a really hurtful email. I hate the person who sent me that. I must be pretty worthless for someone to talk to me that way. I think I'll send a response so loaded with invective and syntactic daggers this person will never bother me again.' I read an email that disturbs me … I feel mobilized in my gut … my body responds first … then my thinking alters. This is a trivial example of the ordinary junction that previously would set in motion a chain of events that would lead to me needing to drink, or use or 'act out' – the kind of everyday challenge that I needed an addictive supplement to tackle. Now that I have made a decision not to live that life, I have to recommit to it every time I encounter an event that triggers my old

> 'If you're like me, you'll begin to see that you have learned to live with dissatisfaction, always vaguely aggrieved, believing there is nothing better out there for you. There is.'

way of thinking. This happens more than you might think, or notice; it happens to me all the time. I rely on the support of other people who work 12 Step programs. So when I get a troubling email and the accompanying troubling feeling, I call someone and ask for help. This tiny act of ingenuity disrupts, enormously (!) my previous model of behaviour, which was 'Feel, Think (maybe!), Act' – the compulsion is ingrained and barely conscious so I have to be vigilant to spot the opportunity to change direction.

My life in active addiction was an unexamined matrix of disturbances held at bay by addictive behaviour. The stimulus–response relationship between me, myself and the world was like this: 'I'm lonely – have sex', 'I'm sad – get drunk', 'I'm bored – eat a cake.' It probably wasn't even that articulate. It was, pre-Step 1, unconscious. Once I had 'admitted I had a problem', drinking and drugs and the impulse to use them were under observation. When I 'came to believe' there was another way to live, this gave me pause, a moment to consider. When I 'made a decision to turn over my will', that meant that when the impulse to use came I conceded that my mental processes were no longer to be trusted. I had to ask for help.

That meant in the early days of my recovery I was continually on the phone to someone with more clean time than me blurting out pleas and gut-felt laments, basically the result of being in a world with other people in it, newly removed from the insulation of active addiction. I have never found it easy to cope with being on our planet, with my spitting, ever-evolving visceral currents and the mad erratic sting of human relationships. I live on an uncertain and volatile circuit. I lived without a program. People are always telling you, 'There's no guide book to being human', but there are loads. The problem, I think, is in translation. How do I make the complex King James, desert books and lurid and beautiful texts of India sing to me in my solitude? How can we, accustomed to living in five-second slices of mindless life, reach back through millennia to hold hands with Vishnu or sit in acceptance with the Buddha? In the world I'm from, no one suggested that anything other than material means could provide me with a solution: Get a job! Do some exercise! You need a nice girlfriend! A hobby! More friends! A palm-held device! An upgrade! Lose a few pounds! No one said, let go of all this, look within, there is no real power in the world of things, only distraction and pleasure.

I have heard 12 Step support groups referred to as a cult and it could be argued that any group with a system of beliefs is a cult. In working a 12 Step program I don't feel like I've joined a cult, but that I've been liberated from one. The cult that told me that I'm not enough, that I need to be famous to be of value, that I need to have money to live a worthwhile life, that I should affiliate, associate and identify on the basis of colour and class, that my role in life is to consume, that I was to live in a darkness only occasionally lit up by billboards and screens, always framing the smiling face of someone trying to sell me something. Sell me phones and food and prejudice, low cost and low values, low-frequency thinking. We are in a cult by default. We just can't see it because its boundaries lie beyond our horizons.

If you're like me, you'll begin to see that you have learned to live with dissatisfaction, always vaguely aggrieved, believing there is nothing better out there for you. There is. I adjusted to misery and medicated myself with drugs. Alone there was no way out, in the culture I was from with the beliefs that I had, there was no way I could change.

No way. Until I made a decision to turn my life and will over to something other than me, what I sometimes call the 'Ulterior Realm', the unified truth between constant mutations or 'the care of God' as I 'understand God'.

Unlike most cults, a 12 Step program tells you to choose your own concept of a Higher Power. My understanding of God, before I got clean, was rather pejorative. That God was an abstract authority icon used to placate the many so that the few could act with impunity. Or that God was a necessary placeholder for the mysteries of being while we waited for science to explain everything. Or that it was just an irrelevant attempt to get me to be moral, like *Blue Peter* or an AIDS awareness leaflet.

I was invited to review my attitude to the idea of transcendent conscious phenomena when my silly little life lay in tatters amidst the dregs. This was a tentative process. While I could admit my life was a mess, I wasn't yet willing to yield all of my theories. 'I'm still clever,' I thought, 'I've worked hard on some of these beliefs.' What is a belief really? *A thought, in your mind, that you like having.* If you like having it, it must be of benefit, it either improves your life or helps you to rationalize how bad your life is. I can't think of another reason to have a belief.

Step 3 is a chance for us to review how our beliefs are working for us. Whether the beliefs are 'pulling their weight'. In Step 2 we 'came to believe' that things could be better, now we are confronted with how that is likely to be achieved, and here's the knockout punch, it isn't likely to be by repeating what we were already doing.

Let's consider you personally for a moment. You've bought this book or gone to the trouble of stealing it and you deserve a little attention. You've admitted you have a problem. You believe change is possible.

Are you now going to cling to the idea that it is you that's going to instantiate that change? Using what? Your brain? Your scheming and insight? I'm afraid to tell you that these are the very qualities that have deposited you in this jam. Don't feel bad about it, I bet you're not as fucked up as I was. I was reluctant to let go of my plan, in spite of its evident inefficiency. 'Me and the plan just need a bit more time', I used to think, a bit more time and a bottle of wine, a bit more time and one more pipe, a bit more time and a slice of cake, a bit more time and a threesome, for luck.

My plan operated in confinement. My plan walked with heavy steps in a deep well-trodden trench dug by the years of unconscious trudging.

How about another plan?
No way!
Sigh. Let's look at Step 1 again.
Okay.
So you see, you're fucked, look. You admitted it.
Yes.
Okay, that's very good. Now Step 2, it could be better than this couldn't it?
Yes, we did agree that, yes.
Excellent. Now, very slowly, what is it about your plan, in your head, using your brain, the brain you've always had, that you think is going to, this time, more than all the other times, which we saw in Step 1, never, ever work, what is it about you and 'your plan' that is so hard to let go of?
Well, it's my plan, I thought of it.
And that is very nice. But it doesn't work. We've proved it. I tell you what, how about a compromise?
Oh yes please, I love compromises.
Why don't we try a new plan, just for today, and if you don't

like it, you can go back to your old plan?
  Oh okay then.

Ha! Got him.

Just for today would you be willing to consider a different plan? Would you be prepared to follow guidance, to accept help? Are you willing to accept that your previous way has let you down? It isn't your fault. You needn't beat yourself up for not having had a better plan, just let it go. At this point the possibility for real change is emerging, real freedom, everything that has been sought through ineffectual facsimiles is going to become available.

Step 3 Exercises: Are you, on your own, going to 'unfuck' yourself?

Step 3 is about accepting help and relinquishing our plan. Our plan is based on our 'current program', as experienced through our thoughts and feelings. It is a vital shift in perspective that needs to be embraced. You will prevaricate. I do. I feel the surge of will and reclaim the reins of the hedonic chariot.

Let's go through these questions together:

- Am I feeling unsatisfied, limited, empty or anxious in my relationships? *Yes. I get pissed off with the people I work with. I want more from my romantic partner. My family don't understand me.*
- Do my feelings lead me to make (or not make) decisions, take (or not take) actions, or say (or not say) things that I then regret? *Yes, this is always happening. My feelings surge up and dominate me. I'm always thinking, 'I shouldn't've done that', or 'I wish I'd said this'.*
- Am I suffering from misery, depression, unhappiness or low self-worth? *Yes. I feel all of these things. I can see why you're querying the efficacy of my plan.*
- Am I suffering from anxiety, doubt or perfectionism? Am I projecting imaginary future scenarios then worrying about them? *Yes. I'm afraid much of the time. I do try to anticipate the future, hoping that I can somehow manage it.*
- Is it becoming clear to me that my plan is not working? *Yes. If I am this discontent in this many areas my plan does need to change.*
- Is it clear that I need a new plan that is not sourced from my own head and drives if I am to find fulfilment? *Yes. I can see that I need a new way, a new path. I have exhausted my self-divined methods.*
- This plan of mine is like a mind virus of self-obsession. Can I surrender it? Am I open to a different plan? Am I open to being guided? *Yes! How many more times? Tell me what to do!*

We are trapped in a way of 'being' that is not working. Here are some categories which will help us amend our perspective. We can usually identify the root of pain and spiritual discomfort within these areas:

1 **Pride** (what *I think* you think about me)
2 **Self-esteem** (what I think about myself)
3 **Personal relations** (the script I give others)
4 **Sexual relations** (as above, pertaining to sex)
5 **Ambitions** (what I want in life, my overall vision of my 'perfect' self)
6 **Security** (what I need to survive)
7 **Finances** (money and how it affects my feelings)

It is good to be reminded of these categories as we undertake Step 4.

4

Write down all the things that are fucking you up or have ever fucked you up and don't lie, or leave anything out.

Step 4: We made a searching and fearless moral inventory of ourselves.

I avoided Step 4 like I owed it money. Fuck that. Fuck it on so many levels, most obviously, I just cannot be bothered to sit and write out in a stringent and formalized fashion, every single bloody thing I can remember that has caused me to be disturbed, to have an emotion, energy in motion, a twitch, a glitch, a mental emotional spasm, sculpting 'the new normal'. Every time I felt some kid at school slight me, or a teacher didn't like me, or a grandparent wasn't 'Disney' enough, or when girls didn't fancy me, or I lost a fight, or West Ham lost, or another kid in another continent got a part in a film, or it rained, or a birthday cake caught fire, or my mum laughed too loudly at a party, or a train was late, or I'm too fat, or my dick's not big enough. The list goes on and it all seems like a lot of effort until you remember Steps 1, 2 and 3 – 'I'm fucked. It could improve. I better do what I'm told.' Plus how much time have I given over to watching TV or staring out of windows or pursuing pointless relationships or looking at my Twitter mentions? Those hours all add up and are sadly deducted from the overall life total. They are not a break from life, these 'harmless' distractions, they are life. They are life and they are death.

If you want me to actually quantify it, time wise, it took me five years and two days to do Step 4. Five years to not do it and two days to do it. That's it, two days. For two days I wrote and wrote and remembered and remembered and I was thorough. I put anything that crossed my mind down on that list.

Most people can't be arsed to make a personal inventory. I was clean and sober for five years based on the first three steps and the support of other addicts. The point of this inventory is to assess and understand the many complex, interconnecting beliefs that I carry around, that underwrite my behaviours, patterns and habits. It was at this point in my program that I began to plainly recognize that my substance abuse was the symptom of a more profound problem.

I was instructed by my mentor (someone who has worked the Steps already) to write down everyone that I knew between the ages of zero and five years old, then five and ten, ten and fifteen, fifteen and twenty and so on. Between five and ten there were a smattering of friends, family and neighbours; life was simple then. As I grew older more institutions and individuals came into my life and do you know what? I had a grudge of some kind against pretty much all of them.

Once I'd been through my entire life writing down anyone I could remember or any institution or object or indeed concept that I had a 'resentment' against the next phase began. I divided up an exercise book into four columns, like this:

I Resent	Because	This Affects My	My Part
_____	_____	_____	_____

In the left-hand column I put the person, place or thing against which I had a resentment. In my case it was likely my dear ol' mum. That's right, you have to be entirely honest and start at the beginning, so down she goes: Mum. Then the second column, into this I put the 'cause' of my resentment: for getting cancer when I was seven. It doesn't matter that it's not my mum's fault that she got cancer; this process is not about justification or correct allocation of blame. It is an inventory of feelings, feelings that are muddled and misunderstood and form a matrix of discontent that in the addict personality lead to destructive and unconscious behaviours. This step is about bringing unconscious behaviour to light. In the third column we write what it is in us that is affected.

As we saw in the last exercise these are:

Pride – what *I think* you think about me

Self-esteem – what I think about myself

Personal relations – the script I give others

Sexual relations – as above, pertaining to sex

Ambitions – what I want in life, my overall vision of my 'perfect' self

Security – what I need to survive

Finances – money and how it affects my feelings

So with this resentment, against my mum, which I had unconsciously harboured for twenty years until I got clean, then another five until I undertook this inventory, I look at the effects it has had on me.

Pride – does it affect the way others think about me? Not clearly, so I don't put *P* (we can abbreviate to the initial) in the third column.

Self-esteem – do I feel guilty or ashamed about it? Actually yes – because another relative told me (and I believed) that my mother being sick was my fault because I was bad. (Which incidentally is a whole other resentment in itself that will have to be worked through separately.) So *SE* goes in the third column.

Personal relations – my mum getting cancer is not how I saw the script for my relationship with her panning out. So this area was affected. Many subsequent relationships with women were also affected by this aberration. I have been overly reliant on women ever since. So *PR* goes into the third column.

The next area is *Sexual relations*. Now we don't need to reanimate the corpse of dear Sigmund Freud to deduce that my subsequent sexual relations have in some way been affected by my relationship with my mother and this illness and my resentment about it are defining aspects of that relationship, so *SR* goes in the column.

This in turn affects my *Ambitions* to have a normal and happy domestic life so *A* goes in too.

My *Security*, my requirement for basic domestic fulfilment was also, for a long time, affected by this resentment so that too goes in.

Finances, the final category, were not affected in any obvious way so there is no need for *F* to be in the third column.

So, at this stage the resentment table would look like this:

I Resent	Because	This Affects My	My Part
Mum	For getting cancer	SE, PR, SR, A, S	

Now my analysis of myself and my own psyche and its various attachments and consequences is obviously subjective. That is why this process is undertaken with the guidance and experience of a mentor. The fifth step is ultimately about sharing this inventory with at least one other person, ideally the one who guided you through its construction and it is this confession that helps to realign your perspective of these events. In a sense we re-write our past. We change

> We have to let go of our opinion of how other people, places and things ought to be. My mum, my girlfriend Laura and the government of North Korea are not obliged to moderate their reality in accordance with my whims.'

our narrative. We reprogram ourselves. There is no objective history, this we know, only stories. Our character is the result of this story we tell ourselves about ourselves, and the process of inventorying breaks down the hidden and destructive personal grammar that we have unwittingly allowed to govern our behaviour.

At this point in the exercise we are reminded that we have to let go of our opinion of how other people, places and things ought to be. My mum, my girlfriend Laura and the government of North Korea are not obliged to moderate their reality in accordance with my whims. If I make my happiness contingent on them behaving in a certain way, I am fucked. I have to petition the universe, my innermost self, God, or whatever it is that I believe might be more powerful than me, to adjust my view – the view that my feelings have a meaningful bearing on the external world. We don't trouble ourselves unduly with soteriology – whether or not sacrifice or practice on the human plane reaches supernatural or materially inaccessible realms – it's too bloody complex.

Basically we accept that the world is the way it is, but we ourselves can change. What we learn from the information in the fourth column is most likely to facilitate change. The anonymous sage that formulated the version I use suggests that we ask ourselves the following questions with any resentment. I'll use my previous example of my mum's illness to demonstrate.

1 Where did I make a Mistake?
With my mum and her illness I have made a mistake in imagining that she has any agency over her own cancer, also in holding on to this belief for thirty years.

2 Where have I been Selfish?
I have allowed myself to become insular in my self-preservation because of the fear that I would lose my mum.

3 Where was I Dishonest?
I used her illness to extract sympathy, advantage and guilt from others, knowing it was a kind of collateral.

4 Where was I Self-seeking?
I wasn't really self-seeking in a way that was problematic.

5 Where was I Afraid?
This is usually the most revealing question and the data we gather from this line of enquiry for me personally holds the key to freedom and change. Behind our damaged perceptions there is usually a fear that pertains to a core belief. This core belief is a key line in the code of our personal misery: if we expose, address and alter it, we can be free. So, behind my resentment at my mum's illness is my fear that I will be left alone and that I can't take care of myself. This false belief is present in many of my most destructive behaviours. My guess is that it will be there in yours too.

6 Where am I to Blame?
In this example I am not to blame in a way that is distinct from what's been covered by the other questions.

7 Where am I at Fault?
This question asks us to look at our 'defective characteristics'

which are usually present when we are resentful. Some examples of defective characteristics are: Arrogance, Avarice, Contempt, Cowardice, Cruelty, Disobedience, Distrust, Domination, Envy, Gluttony, Impatience, Impenitence, Indifference, Intolerance, Jealousy, Lack of discipline, Laziness, Lust, Malice, Over-ambition, Over-sensitivity, Presumption, Pride, Prudery, Pugnacity, Retaliation, Self-pity, Sentimentality, Shame (hurt pride), Snobbery, Timidity, Vanity, Violation of confidence, Wastefulness. Usually when I am disturbed, fearful or disconnected, I am exhibiting some of these traits. In this resentment Self-pity, Sentimentality, Intolerance and Laziness are all present.

8 Where was I Wrong?

This crosses over categorically with Mistakes and Blame but is there to specifically identify other people that have been wronged by your behaviour. In this case my mum has been harmed by my subsequent unavailability. So I make a note of that as it will become relevant later when we reach Step 8.

The 'fearless and thorough' consideration of all these questions ensures no data will be left uncovered if we are honest, open and willing. The completed table for this resentment looks like this:

I Resent	Because	This Affects My	My Part	
Mum	For getting cancer	SE, PR, SR, A, S	**1**	Mistakes: Y
			2	Selfishness: Y
			3	Dishonesty: Y
			4	Self-seeking: N
			5	Fear: Y
			6	Blame: N
			7	Fault: Y
			8	Wrong: Y

> 'If you're chugging through life in a job you kind of dislike, a relationship that you are detached from, eating to cope, staring at Facebook, smoking and fruitlessly fantasizing, you can sit glumly on that conveyor belt of unconscious discontent until it deposits you in your grave.'

The completed table acts as an aide-memoire when you share its contents with the person guiding you through this process, or if you are doing it remotely without guidance (which I wouldn't advise), the person you choose to do your Step 5 confession with.

After you have completed this process for twenty representative resentments that give a clear depiction of your life's patterns and habits – likely a few ex-partners, family members, anyone that has severely transgressed against you, school bullies, grandparents, strangers, Christmas, monarchs, road users and Facebook – you will have a clearer understanding of the coordinates of your world view.

Now it is time for our specific Fear Inventory. Go through your entire list looking specifically at the fears in the fourth column. Here is the method for arriving at a core fear as opposed to a superficial one. You have to chase the fear down to its essence like you're hunting a tenacious mosquito.

For example, I might feel afraid of going for a job interview. Behind this is the superficial fear 'I might not get the job', so what?

'Well, if I don't get the job, I won't have enough money.'

Again, what's behind that fear?

'If I don't have enough money, I will be poor, if I am poor I won't be able to look after myself.' So, the core fear in this instance is – 'I cannot look after myself'.

Or perhaps you are resentful because you asked someone on a date and they knocked you back, or someone rejected your friend request on social media. 'I am afraid that this person doesn't find me attractive.' So what? 'I am afraid that no one finds me attractive.' So what? 'I am afraid that I will never find anyone to be with me.' So what? 'I am afraid of being alone' – core fear, being alone.

Isn't it a good thing to know about yourself? That you are going through life requesting friends on Facebook and asking people on dates driven by an existential fear that you will always be alone? When were you planning to address that? Is your plan to go through your (finite) human life motivated by unexamined dread? Is that your plan? And you wonder why you're fucking nervous?! At the heart of so much activity and interaction is deep and unaddressed fear. We have to expose it! We have to amend it! We need help! Thank God you read this book you lunatic. Now you obviously can't undertake this process alone, using your limited and highly biased world view to come up with a solution, especially as it's your head that got you into this dilemma. When I undertook this process it was with men who were further down the path than me. You will also require help.

The first three steps have their fair share of mysticism. The first step and its principle of honest self-appraisal and surrender, the second with its call for hope, the third with the outlandish requirement for faith, if this is challenging for you then the fourth step will provide ontological respite but requires great practical effort.

Steps 4 and 5 are the inescapable admin steps. Up until this point you can get by on agreeing with some abstract concepts: that you are powerless over people, places and things; that when you exert control your life, your experience of life, becomes unmanageable; that it is possible that there is another way; that the way you live isn't the only possible way; that by conceding authority you will access new data.

It was obvious I was powerless over heroin. It was clear that the people that taught me this program had found another way. It was as plain as day that I needed to be taught new skills. In the case of straightforward addictions you get to work a kindergarten version of this program. The object, the symbol, is clearly defined. It isn't easy. No one likes going through withdrawal or delirium tremens, but it does have the advantage of being easily identifiable. The problem of denial is hopefully easier to confront. If you're chugging through life in a job you kind of dislike, a relationship that you are detached from, eating to cope, staring at Facebook, smoking and fruitlessly fantasizing, you can sit glumly on that conveyor belt of unconscious discontent until it deposits you in your grave.

We take stock of all of the beliefs and resentments that populate our conscious experience of the world. If this is done thoroughly we begin to see where our explicit beliefs intersect with our unconscious beliefs. An example: my former belief that I needed to sleep with a lot of women, when unscrutinized could pose as 'culturally acceptable', 'cool', 'fun', 'aspirational', 'harmless'. Once thoroughly inventoried this behaviour was exposed as 'desperate', 'pitiful', 'toxic', 'lonely'. The behaviour had been designed or adopted as a strategy to prevent pain. When you check Facebook, or browse to consume, or obsess about going out, what unconscious motivation lurks, unqueried? Obviously you don't know, we are after all dealing with THE UNCONSCIOUS. It's likely the architecture of your belief contains pillars such as 'There's nothing wrong with it', 'Everyone does it' and 'There is nothing better I could be doing'. This will be challenged, possibly overwhelmed by the first three steps. In Step

4 we get a detailed understanding of how these codes combine and perpetuate certain behaviours. In Step 5 we begin to experience the revelation that is only found through connection to another. For me this process challenged, for the first time, a great many of my defining yet unexamined beliefs: 'No one understands me', 'No one loves me', 'I am alone', 'I am worthless', 'I am different to everyone else', 'I cannot be loved'. These constitute cumbersome personal baggage. Every time I iterate those beliefs I feel the abdominal pang of their power and the tearfulness of this condition.

Back to you. Are there things about yourself which you have never told anyone? Way back upon the creaky floors of your childhood, in your solitude, the shadows of your private mind, the things you've done and said and thought that compound and contain you: shameful things, sexual things, often solitary acts, but sometimes not, sometimes agonizing stabs of cruelty you've inflicted on people you love, or the moments where reality itself seemed to tear as they looked into your eyes and told you 'you are nothing'. And for a moment you stand there adjusting to the pain, the pain that someone could say that to you, and what that must mean about who you are. Or what it means to be cruel, to have hurt someone, to feel the cords of love that bind, split and flail and to fall away, into yourself, engulfed but absolutely alone. And you do what humans do: you accept and you adapt. You build the pain into the story of who you are until it isn't pain anymore, it's just another piece of who you are.

I was touched as a child and I felt the warping, like flexed glass, not entirely unpleasant, it was after all attention, but I knew it was a glitch, like a memory I was waiting to have, like a stone on the path that I knew I would not pass but pause to pick up and carry with me, uneasily in my pocket. Finding ways to incorporate this transgression into my understanding of the world, stitching it into the fabric of my understanding. 'Mum is ill a lot.' 'They say I am bad.' 'My dad does not like me.' 'I am not safe.' 'I don't like school.' 'I don't belong.' 'People don't like me.' 'I made Mummy ill.' 'I am bad.' Until chocolate and porn and self-harm seem like sanctuary from the gentle unbearable pain. And as we walk along we collect and collate the familiar, the path appears before our feet as we walk and we move further from home until we are too far away to recall that we ever even had a home.

The process is designed to illuminate and it ought to be thorough and exhaustive but it needn't be repetitive. I have learned that from a limited grid of behaviours, thoughts and feelings I cast and project the apparent variety of my chaotic life. When analysed I can see how there is usually a simple pattern creating this apparent mayhem.

I did this under guidance. Having completed your inventory to the best of your ability you then 'share it with God, yourself and another human being'. This is usually your mentor or guide, or at any rate someone you trust who is further down the path you hope to walk. If at this point of the book you haven't identified sufficiently with one of the issues for which there is a global 'fellowship' with a strong online presence – like alcoholism, drug addiction, sex addiction, eating disorders, codependency, relationship problems, smoking, debt, work addiction, gambling, spending, technology addiction – then my suggestion would be that you find someone from one of those movements who identifies with your particular, or rather more amorphous problem and undergo this process with them. The possibility of founding your own group also exists, based on proximity of condition or location. It is my belief and indeed prayer that we will form support communities that cover all issues all over the world. That these communities will form the basis for our continuing social evolution towards a society founded on a harmonious relationship between the inner and outer world and love and support of one another until social systems based on economics and outmoded hierarchies become obsolete. I'll just drop that in there.

Step 4 Exercises: Write down all the things that are fucking you up or have ever fucked you up and don't lie, or leave anything out.

Have a look at the table on p272-3. In the first column we put the thing that has pissed us off. Is it Donald Trump or some kid who bullied you at school? (It could be the same person, though I've heard Donald Trump was nice at school.)

What I mean is, it could be a major geo-political issue or it could be that someone cut you up while you were driving.

In the second column we put why we are pissed off: 'They cut me up' or 'They aren't acknowledging the energy crisis' or 'They preferred my sister' or 'They abused me' – nothing is too big or too small. My Step 4 had both extremes on it.

One way to ensure thoroughness is to write a list of everyone you can remember throughout your life: aged zero to five, five to ten, ten to fifteen … until the present day. I could think of things that pissed me off about people that I had forgotten existed. It all went in the inventory.

In the third column we look at which area of our life is affected by this perceived (or real) transgression. Is it Pride, Self-esteem, etc.? Some resentments affect all seven areas, some affect one. If none are affected – what the hell is your problem?!

Here once again are the seven areas – only put the ones that apply to your resentment into the third column.

1 Pride
2 Self-esteem
3 Personal relations
4 Sexual relations
5 Ambitions
6 Security
7 Finances

In the powerful and revealing fourth column we identify where we participated in this problem.

1 **Mistakes** – what could I have done differently here?
2 **Selfishness** – have I sneakily been selfish without acknowledging it?
3 **Dishonesty** – am I being straight up here?
4 **Self-seeking** – am I after some dumb selfish thing that maybe I need to let go of?
5 **Fear** – what fear lies beneath this resentment, underwriting it? That I am unlovable? That I will end up alone?
6 **Blame** – am I in any way to blame for this?
7 **Fault** – which 'defects of character' am I exhibiting?
8 **Wrong** – have I damaged anyone? Will I later owe amends, apologies and restitution to someone?

Again, it isn't necessary to put something for each question but you will find that you are yourself participating in the pain that you harbour, that's why you harbour it. It's not about allocation of blame (we aren't in court!) it's about moving to a different perspective where we can live in peace.

Having been exhaustive with the list of people you have known and resentments you can recall, select twenty that you believe define you: familial relationships, romantic partnerships, jobs, situations. With each item on this list of twenty complete the four-column process.

Obviously it should be the twenty resentments that most play on your mind. The milestones and dominant coordinates of your psyche. In my opinion, and in the creed of these steps as written, it is considered crucial that you undertake this process under the guidance of someone who has previously completed it, with whom you have no conflicting connection. By which I mean, not someone you are in love with, or have a long-running secret or seething feud with.

5

Honestly tell someone trustworthy about how fucked you are.

Step 5: We admitted to God, to ourselves and to another human being the exact nature of our wrongs.

The first time I did Step 5 it was with my second mentor. I identified primarily as a drug addict and he as an alcoholic but it made no difference, the feelings we were dealing with seemed to be uniform. I had fifty or sixty pages of A4 paper covered with dense writing and dense feelings. Some of the 'resentments' I had written were so appalling and shameful I thought I was severed from redemption forever. Some were so petty and insignificant I was embarrassed that I even remembered them. One by one I read them out, admitting 'my wrongs' to God (Ultimate Self? Pure Consciousness? Uncaused Awareness?), myself and another human being. As it transpired we were in a beautiful house in Malibu. I was about to start work on the film *Get Him to the Greek*. I was giddy and elated but somehow still dissatisfied and after five years of trundling along as a sex addict, I was now willing to surrender further. It was a beautiful environment to be working in but that was irrelevant in the sense that the majority of my time, maybe fourteen hours a day, was spent hunched over the pages of this inventory, untangling memories and committing them to the page.

I had chosen my mentor because he was a charming and articulate madman. I could tell he knew the darkness and he had ten years' more experience than I did. He was an empathetic and kind man, but not a sage or a shaman, not a blanket-draped, white-eyed, mountain-dwelling yogi. Just a drunk who had found a way not to drink, one day at a time. Like me, like you, he was still mad but the program is not mad. The program is a map out of madness for anyone who wants to follow it. I recited the list. Column 1, *I resent*, column 2, *the resentment itself*, column 3, *how it affected me*.

This recitation had an impact that for me transcended rational understanding. To hear myself air all these secret fears and hatreds, these insecurities, punctured the membrane of isolation I had lived in. To see the pattern of repeated behaviours that dominated my life was enlightening. I began to see how I already lived by a program. A repeated pattern is a program. The confession itself though has a profound effect, which can be best understood by returning to the wording of the step: 'We admitted to God, to ourselves and to another human being the exact nature of our wrongs'. Confession returned me to the wholeness of my self and the wholeness of the world. It was restorative. The compartmentalizing and separateness was undone. I'd never before acknowledged the role of fear in my life, that many of my behaviours were unwittingly governed by fear: that my fear of rejection led me to seek out relationships that precluded real intimacy; that my fear of inadequacy meant that even friendships with other men were fraught and unconsciously guarded; that my fear of being alone meant I bound people to me who were not positive influences in my life. Much of the revelatory information did not concern substance misuse at all. It concerned the working of my heart and my emotions. If epiphany is the revelation of essence, then this process induces an epiphany of sorts. When I saw written out in my own hand the codes and patterns that had led me into continual conflict and confusion I was astonished that it could be understood so formulaically. It was a great revelation to learn that my problem was not alcohol, heroin, crack, bulimia or sex but a twisted system of beliefs brought on by trauma and shame that had become the basis of my unconscious program for living.

This is a beautiful step. For me it spelled the end of the loneliness and isolation I have always felt and that I have continually tried to medicate against. Do you have it too? A feeling of worthlessness and inadequacy? A fear of death and of being alone? When I first read my inventory of mistakes, fear and hatred to another person, he melted

> 'Suddenly my fraught and freighted childhood became reasonable and soothed. "My mum was doing her best, so was my dad." Yes, people made mistakes but that's what humans do and I am under no obligation to hoard these errors and allow them to clutter my perception of the present.'

them away with identification and compassion. Loathing of my own body. Hatred of people I 'ought' to love. Shame around abuse as a child. In each case he reached across the moat of toxic yet ignored pain and isolation and told me it was okay, that he too had similar fears and cited direct examples.

In undertaking this process you are declaring an intention to change. Confession has its place in most faiths and is of course the bedrock of psychiatrist-led psychoanalysis. Freud and Jung listened as their patients evacuated a lifetime of perceived malady. In the original 12 Step texts it is suggested that you undertake the confession with the person who has guided you through the program thus far or a cleric of some kind or a medical professional. Really the primary qualification ought to be that it is someone that understands the spirit of the exercise. I wouldn't recommend doing it with a park bench drunk or a *Daily Mail* columnist. They may bite back.

My mentor sat and smoked and listened hour after hour while I unloaded the deadening burden. Occasionally we would reach a 'big one', child abuse, my mother's sickness, my feelings of abandonment by my father, my obsessive promiscuity, painful romantic relationships, opportunities lost through drugs, and I'd steel myself. Sometimes I'd skip through pages of trivial grudges barely pausing. He would sometimes stop and analyse a resentment that I had not regarded as especially significant and point out a pattern, or identify himself. The main thing was there was nothing I said that was too terrible or too trivial to shock or bore him. He identified throughout and through this practical communication an unexpected thing happened: the veil of separation that I had lived my life behind lifted. The tense disconnectedness that I had always felt lifted. It is commonly understood that the opposite of addiction is connection. That in our addictive behaviours we are trying to achieve the connection. Think of it: the bliss of a hit or a drink or of sex or of gambling or eating, all legitimate drives gone awry, all a reach across the abyss, the separateness of 'self', all an attempt to redress this disconnect.

There is humility in confession. A recognition of flaws. To hear myself say out loud these shameful secrets meant I acknowledged my flaws. I also for the first time was given the opportunity to contextualize anew the catalogue of beliefs and prejudices, simply by exposing them to another, for the first time hearing the words 'Yes, but have you looked at it this way?' This was a helpful step in gaining a new perspective on my past, and my past was a significant proportion of who I believed myself to be. It felt like I had hacked into my own past. Unravelled all the erroneous and poisonous information I had unconsciously lived with and lived by and with necessary witness, the accompaniment of another man, reset the beliefs I had formed as a child and left unamended through unnecessary fear.

Suddenly my fraught and freighted childhood became reasonable and soothed. 'My mum was doing her best, so was my dad.' Yes, people made mistakes but that's what humans do, and I am under no obligation to hoard these errors and allow them to clutter my perception of the present. Yes, it is wrong that I was abused as a child but there is no reason for me to relive it, consciously or unconsciously, in the way I conduct my adult relationships. My perceptions of reality, even my own memories, are not objective or absolute, they are a biased account and they can be altered. It is possible to reprogram your mind. Not alone, because a tendency, a habit, an addiction will always reassert by its own invisible momentum, like a tide. With this program, with the support of others, and with this mysterious power, this new ability to change, we achieve a new perspective, and a new life.

I learned that I had no need to feel ashamed, that I could make amends for the wrongs I had done, that I could address the fear I had always fled, that I could re-evaluate my feelings of worthlessness. Why did I choose to live in a punitive version of reality for so long? Because I was unaware that there was a choice and I was unwilling to do the work. But if you think about it any version of a personally authored reality is highly suspect because we are seldom taking into account the cosmic vastness in which we live and the microscopic grace that carries us through life. I don't wake up in the morning and think, 'Wow, I'm on a planet in the Milky Way, in infinite space, bestowed with the gift of consciousness, which I did not give myself, with the gift of language, with lungs that breathe and a heart that beats, none of which I gave myself, with no concrete understanding of the Great Mysteries, knowing only that I was born and will die and nothing of what's on either side of this brief material and individualized glitch in the limitless expanse of eternity and, I feel, I feel love and pain and I have senses, what a glorious gift! I can relate, and create and serve others or I can lose myself in sensuality and pleasure. What a phenomenal mystery!' Most days I just wake up feeling a bit anxious and plod a solemn, narrow path of survival, coping. 'I'll have a coffee', 'I'll try not to reach for my phone as soon as I stir, simpering and begging like a bad dog at a table for some digital tidbit, some morsel of approval, a text, that'll do.'

I have learned through the process of inventorying that it is possible to intervene in my thinking, that I have a choice. In the past a lustful thought led to a lustful act. In inventorying and sharing I have gained some perspective, my thoughts are in fact the first layer of the 'outside world'. I am not my thoughts. I observe my thoughts. So now if I start thinking about sex, on a good day, I will spot it early enough in the process to make a choice. 'Do I want to peruse this avenue? This boulevard lined with trees apple-laden with old temptation? Is this going to be good for me? Or should I observe my breath, slow down, pick up the phone and share with someone I trust, that my mind, my naughty little mind, was about to fling my life off a cliff for fifteen minutes of mild amusement.'

Confession it seems is ritualized and recognized by most cultures. The version of confession practised in Steps 4 and 5 is functional, modern and connected. The inevitability of erring, the dilemma that all who live encased in flesh incur irascible drives and urges. I unloaded it all and I knew myself better. I knew what I was and what I was not. I knew it was okay to be imperfect and that I was lovable in my imperfection, holy, whole, complete and perfect, free from conflict and contradiction.

For about an hour.

Then my mentor flew back to England and the estate agent who had rented us the house for a week called and said a couple who had booked the house for a wedding next week wanted to come and have a look round. Not unreasonable you might think, certainly not for someone who had just had the soul-cleansing experience of Step 5. Well let me tell you what I told that estate agent, 'You cannot bring anyone here. I booked it for privacy and I am going to have privacy. I am barricading the gates and if I hear the buzzer go, I will release all the goats and chickens' (there were goats and chickens) 'and flood the place'. The estate agent was so distressed that he (I hope it was a he) called the Sheriff of Malibu (can there have been a less threatening law enforcement officer in history?) and I had to be smuggled off the premises to hide out at a beach cabana until the whole crazy affair blew over. So you see, I am still quite human, quite flawed, but at least I was able to put the estate agent onto my next inventory and I was able to clearly identify which 'defects of character' had blown up and caused this whole unfortunate business. I still haven't apologized to the goats and chickens.

The last time I did Step 5 it was in a more manageable form. I identified twenty resentments that characterized my problems and I read them to three different people. Because I have fourteen and a half years in recovery, I know a lot of people with more time than me and more experience. In the purest (and likely still the best after dozens of translations and reiterations) *Alcoholics Anonymous Big Book* it suggests doing your Step 5 with a doctor, clergyman or a stranger. That sounds a bit eccentric to me, and possibly a waste of a hard-won GP appointment. The important thing is that it ought to be someone who will understand the spirit of what you are doing, which is exposing your truest, previously concealed self in a way that leaves no room for deception of yourself or anyone else. I would recommend someone who already has a 12 Step program or is seriously tuned in through some other ideology. If I had to pick a well-known person it would be Oprah, Eckhart Tolle or the Dalai Lama. But basically anyone with a 12 Step program would be okay. Just don't splurge your deepest emotional secrets on someone who dislikes you or loves you too much.

There are three points of connection. We must connect to our earthed and ordinary self, a fundamental self-awareness. We equally require a connection to a Higher Self, a quiet, ever-present awareness within, that some may call God. But we must also connect with others. If you're anything like me, this is a difficult prospect. I've never found life among humans easy. I'd rather be flat on my stomach, watching TV in 1980 with *Star Wars* figures, or flat on my back on smack, or lost in a wilderness of unfamiliar limbs, looking for God in strangers' faces. These days though I have many lateral connections with men and women, other men and women like me, who share this condition. I know I would not be able to stay clean and connected to this new way alone. Alone I always return to familiar self-centredness and then self-destruction. I need to be in groups. I need to be one of a number, a member of a community. Nothing about my outward appearance or deliberate behaviour demonstrates this, whether it's my haircut or the way I make a living: solitude, isolation and individualism have been my inner creed. Although this program can be worked alone, in that you could go through this manual in isolation, in a cell, if that's your only option, real change and growth requires a connection to others. Is there a self without dialectic? Who are we when we are alone? We live in our relationships. I have to belong to a community.

When I first did Step 5, I felt the aquarium of isolation crack. When I listen to other men read their inventories, detailed accounts of their pain and shame, I feel my love flow out. I feel warmly connected to them, my innate tendency to self-obsession abates. In these relationships that are built on mutual vulnerability and a willingness to help one another I am invited into unexplored aspects of myself. We live in a society in which we all, as individuals and as nations, compete for resources. We are told this is nature's way. My nature cannot long abide it. I become too lonely, locked within my skin.

I am a different man with the people that give me free counsel. I tell them, 'I can't cope with being me, being in a relationship, being at work, being.' They, using their experience and this program guide me out of the illusion of separateness and misery and back to the connection. When my last great romance combusted and I came fleeing from the inferno, looking for comfort and peace, it is to this community, assembled around the mutual wound, that I turned. Every time I reinvest in the material world as a potential source of happiness I am able to return to them when it fails. When religions talk of idolatry, I feel I know what they are saying; when I make something else, other than my connection to myself, nature and others, my 'idol', my symbol of the divine, I get in trouble. If you take away the bombast, the sense that these edicts are being bellowed down from a purple cloud, 'Don't get too wrapped up in relationships or money' sounds like the sort of thing a grandparent might say. I have an inclination to make these things my salvation.

Before this program and the guidance of others using these principles my M.O. was to either be in a giddy and all-consuming romance or to be distracted by incessant promiscuity. I was using these means to deal with the intensity of feeling I experience. The program provides a technique to manage this intensity, either by increasing serenity or directing the intensity in a manner that is less harmful.

When the relationship could no longer successfully wrangle such intense feeling and it spilled into madness, the people that I work this program with were there. When I made the late night phone calls from strange locations, the places you find yourself after a nocturnal conflict (the lobby of a bizarre country hotel), my mate James was there to talk me down from the ledge. Not literally. 'Bruv, it don't sound like this relationship is working, you wanna chat?' When reviewing the wreckage of the tryst, Jimmy talked me through difficult relationships he'd experienced and gave me a new perspective on the preceding months, and was able to lovingly point out where I had been going wrong. Importantly he observed that the relationship had been embarked on based on an erroneous premise. Through inventory and discussion we could see how I habitually get involved with people on the basis of romantic and escapist drives, rather than earthed, domestic intent. Like most of us, I previously saw romantic love as the last repository for divine intention and worship. I thought that a woman could save me: Miss Right, The One, My True Love. This form of idolatry can call upon centuries of romantic love for support but the idea that another human can 'complete' us is built upon the assumption that we are incomplete, inadequate, flawed. I find this yearning of mine will happily ride upon the tide of romantic love. It is better directed towards a union with a Higher Self and an earnest attempt to connect lovingly with all people. This is what I nurture in the company of other addicts. When addicts meet as a group, no matter what the addiction, we have come together on the basis that we need help and that there is hope. Like a tribe that has a shared wound as their initiation, the people in these movements come together bearing the same scar. We must build more communities like these upon the basis of our mutual need.

I often arrive at a 12 Step support group pugnacious and surly, but as I listen to other people honestly share their pain I feel the protective walls come down. I have attended these groups all over the world and connected with people who at first glance I'd think were a different species. When I think of the solidarity I feel in these groups I have an illustrative image that recurs. Imagine walking down a busy city street, the usual parade of glum staring faces, the anonymous people that we are content to brush past. Or when you sit on public transport and everyone is sallow, reading some rag or imbibing a dire sandwich and only terrorism could bring people together. In these groups that people attend on the basis of mutual need, it is as if you could walk up to these anonymous people on the Tube or city street and they would turn to you and lift their eyes and openly recite the contents of their hearts: 'I feel trapped in my marriage'; 'I've never got over being abused'; 'I am lonely.' With these silent and ubiquitous truths spoken the world is not filled with strangers and grey faces because

I cannot help but love people who know the pain I feel. Even if the tune is distinct, when I hear people honestly speak I know the notes they hear in their hearts are the same notes I hear in mine. That beyond the difference of language is the oneness of language's root.

I have lads that I mentor. I know. They call me up to talk about their problems. I know! And removed from the neurological fugue of 'self' and guided by the map of this program, I can see clearly where they should go and I can help them. And as I hear myself telling them how they should 'let go' or 'meditate' or 'be honest' or 'be grateful' I of course realize the universal truth of simple wisdom naturally applies to my problems. Their gratitude helps my self-esteem: 'I cannot be as worthless as I sometimes feel when these people have such trust in me.'

So when I am rattled by the vicissitudes of ordinary life, I find myself suspended by the positive connections I have made with others all on the basis of a shared wound and help freely given. We expect nothing but truth and support from one another. These connections mean that I do not live solely in a world defined by competition and commerce. I have bonds that are, for want of a better word, spiritual. With the popularization of this program and the technology now available we can reach everyone. My friend Kevin Cahill, who for years ran Comic Relief, told me of a support group for women in an Indian slum where the members discussed spousal abuse and how to survive it and be free from it. He said one woman shared how she confronted her husband and told him how his abuse made her feel, that he wept and pledged to change. Whether he will or not remains open to speculation but Kevin said the other women were inspired and hungry. 'How did you do it? What did he say?' they asked. As he spoke I was amazed how for people in circumstances more extreme than most of us will ever know, the principles of community and support were at work. I feel that this program is a folk philosophy that is always trying to be born, a simple way for us all to relate to ourselves and to one another, to come to terms with the conditions of our lives and our deaths.

When my disease is on me, the loneliness and hopelessness seem real. One of the first measures I can take to alleviate it is to reach out to another addict. I continue to attend support groups because I need to be constantly reminded that my condition, untreated, leads to very destructive behaviours but more importantly that my feelings of despair are not unique to me and that they are temporary. That I am just another human being dealing with life. If we all feel that we are alone, how alone are we? If we all feel worthless then who is the currency of our worth being measured against? Perhaps this program is a personal and social tool that illuminates the truth that religious people have long known and physicists have proven: all the energy that has ever existed has always existed and will always exist. Form and separation are temporary. We are all one.

Step 5 Exercises: Honestly tell someone trustworthy about how fucked you are.

Before beginning this step, ask yourself:

- Have I been entirely honest in this inventory?
- Have I been clear about the motives beneath my behaviour?
- Have I reached into my innermost self and asked for truth to be revealed?
- Am I open to a new truth?
- Am I willing to take full responsibility for my feelings, perceptions and my behaviour?
- Am I willing to fully disclose the most intimate and previously concealed nature of myself to another person?

The person we choose should themselves have undertaken this process and have no investment in our life other than a desire to help us.

If you don't know anyone then go to a 12 Step organization that most closely deals with the specificity of your condition. Attend this support group until you feel comfortable to ask someone. Traditionally it has been acceptable to share your inventory with a cleric of your choosing, a medical professional or even a stranger. That seems nuts to me. I've only ever done it with someone who:

- Has done this before
- I respect and trust (obviously I don't trust anyone, that's one of my problems, but I am willing to change this behaviour)
- I don't expect anything from

People that I consider masters of Step 5 say it should only take two hours and that's why twenty resentments, if done thoroughly, will provide a clear picture of our patterns and problems and the areas that require change.

My Steps 4 and 5 revealed that I am, when in my addiction, selfish, self-centred and think that all my problems will be solved if I get fame, money, power, plaudits, sex and glory. That I think I am some kind of God/Hitler/Genghis Khan/Jesus figure. And that I can't cope with this world and its occupants unless I have a hook-up to a greater source of power than my ego can provide.

When I confessed the details of the trauma I had experienced and the shame that I still felt, when I revealed the things that I never thought I'd tell anybody, I felt relief. I also had to acknowledge my hopelessness, my brokenness, my need to change deeply.

Through the compassion and love of those that I shared with I experienced the power of these principles and the reality of forgiveness, of redemption.

I felt willing to change not just my obvious addictive behaviour but also the patterns, thoughts and feelings that had long underwritten them.

Ask yourself:

- Why am I doing Step 5?
- Why am I doing it with the person that I have chosen?
- What is the function of Step 5?

6

Well that's revealed
a lot of fucked up
patterns. Do you
want to stop it?
Seriously?

Step 6: We were entirely ready to have God remove all these defects of character.

This is a step about healing. When I last sprained my ankle I just sat back in entitled convalescence, drumming my fingers, while some unbidden invisible force took care of it. If this were a phenomenon exclusive to me, I'd be dancing nude in the fountain at Lourdes. Although why bother going, with my miraculous, self-healing ankle? As it is, I fully expect the process of healing on an anatomical level to take place. I know too that it will take place on an emotional level; my shattered heart has pieced itself back together a thousand times. I am aware that in the field of physiology, healing will be improved by following certain measures: rest, good diet, medication. This I mention only to build a bridge of rationality to the metaphysical world, once more.

In truth, the part of the step that deserves our focus is the part that we can control, 'became entirely ready'. Through the process of Steps 4 and 5 we have identified some patterns of behaviour and ways of feeling that are unpleasant and painful. What this step calls for is for us to be ready to change them, to accept that they are not working. This would seem obvious but when I saw the role of the character defect 'Lust' in my life I still wasn't ready to relinquish it. I still sought to justify its presence in my life – 'It's natural', 'It's fun', etc.

The 'Where am I at Fault?' question in the fourth column in our fourth step will be informative here. What are our 'defects of character'? I found this quote in the book *Serenity* very useful:

> As a rule, most defects of character involve some imbalance in the expression of and the experience of our most basic human needs. For example, sexuality and ambition are not bad unless our experiences of those drives are imbalanced or codependent.

If we are addicted to sex or driven by ambition to the point of workaholism, these expressions have become defects we must address. Our sixth step prayers would not be 'Make me asexual' or 'Take away my ambition'. Rather, we might pray, 'Grant me a healthy expression of my sexuality' or 'Channel ambition into enhancing my private life as well as my work life'.

For utility and ease let's assume that prayer is an attempt to petition the Highest Aspect of your being, whether you see that as personal or impersonal. In the examples I've been using, my childhood resentment against my mother or a current resentment against my girlfriend, the 'Faults' in the fourth column would include:

- Self-pity (poor me)
- Self-centredness (my feelings are the most important thing in the world)
- Selfishness (who cares about the other person!)
- Greed (I want more, even though I have so much)
- Lust (misdirected drive towards sexual matters)
- Envy (I want what others have)
- Jealousy (I don't want others taking what is 'mine')
- Pride (I must be treated in accordance with my self-defined protocols)
- Intolerance (people should be better, I say)
- Impatience (hurry up and do it my way)
- Sloth (I can't be bothered)
- Arrogance (be more like me)
- Dishonesty (management of narrative for gain)

Having identified these defects through our inventory we have a decision to make: do we want to continue to operate within these patterns or to transcend them? No one wants to be miserable but few people are willing to do the work required to enact change.

> 'In justifying our misery we recommit
> to it.'

My belief is that we accept our suffering and only attempt to tackle it through outward means. Even having identified Lust as a 'defect', a negative and problematic trait, we don't automatically discard it. 'Lust is natural, I'm entitled to lust, if she had sex more I wouldn't look at porn', all these justifications are obstacles to change. In justifying our misery we recommit to it.

The odyssey of recovery begins in earnest when we become willing to truly change. Not content to rotate the object of our addiction we become 'entirely ready for God to remove our defects of character'.

Yesterday I went to attend a straightforward, and many might think, pleasant meeting with a theatre director and an actress. My girlfriend who is pregnant with our first child needed the car. You can see how the condition 'pregnant with our first child' might automatically qualify her for priority for car use – you're right, it does and even I saw that eventually – and without being told. I just realized it, like a half-wit King Solomon: 'I decree, that you, my life-partner and baby mother in a fifty-fifty decision should get the car.' I did first consider cutting the car in two and seeing whose love for the car was fiercer and more true. Actually, I realized, quickly and unprompted, that this situation demanded that I surrender the vehicle and I nearly barfed on silent self-sacrifice as I capitulated. After she departed I realized I'd left necessary items as ridiculous and diverse as shoes and my wallet in the car so eventually took a taxi instead of the intended train into London, nattering at the Muslim driver initially impatient proddings and incentives and then apologetic conversational offerings, as usual steering the conversation towards God, via impending parenthood. This is an aspect of my program and of course an aspect of my disease.

> Out I go, knowing there's nothing for me there, only young women, who I know, in spite of what I read from their appearance, are human beings like me and have inner lives that roll like a threadbare carpet into painful pasts and uncertain futures.'

Having first hassled Adnan to not look at his phone or procrastinate and get a move on, while eating cold porridge on the back seat, I begin to settle into an awareness of the pointlessness of impatience: a defect and constant of my character, which amounts to me thinking that things should happen more quickly than they do, which is an odd mindset, to have an internal template for what the world should be and then to try to drag the outer world into alignment through terse commentary in Adnan's earhole; it is by any stretch a peculiar philosophy.

I can only suppose that I am overly adrenalized in the first instance and it takes a moment to 'come down', plus I was hungry, and as those material circumstances amend, I open to the secondary but more significant reality that Adnan and I are two men in a car in infinite space on the M4 heading to London; that life is a flash of light in what seems to us to be an unending cosmic darkness; that life is a miracle, a rarity, a wonder and we here are participating in this unknowable mystery. Eventually and not too slowly, all things considered, we arrive at the rehearsal space in South-East London, by now I have chatted merrily to Adnan, never directly saying the words, 'Hey, even though I'm a post-secular affluent white man and you are a Muslim cab driver, trapped here in a locomotive capsule, in a fraught time for people of faith, we are united in our most basic drives and our highest spiritual ambitions,' though that is very much the subtext of what I do say.

And in I go, entirely at the behest of swirling conditions and the rootless distraction that I default to when on the phone and in need of a wee and carrying a cereal bowl and spoon from home, into the advertising agency that siren women giggle me into – once inside this unintended destination I use the loo and marvel at the youth. They seem cast rather than employed by this idealized version of a London ad agency. They are literally playing foosball and drinking bottled beer in their loft-style office and in a corner a pair of properly pigmented beauties play on a games console. What is their actual work I wonder?

They are a creative agency for advertising; they come up with concepts for big brands. That means I suppose they devise attractive stories and symbols to make objects seem desirable beyond what is rational. Attractive in a manner that is fizzily deceptive. I'm only in there for a hundred or so seconds and only because I'm recognizable and while in there, on the phone still to my mate, I am scanning the environment for something to hang on to, for something that means something, not like a person who is drowning, just like a person who is adrift. They are so beautiful, I keep thinking. We are in Southwark so a hundred years ago this building would've been a stinking tannery. Have you ever smelt leather at any point in its cycle other than the delicious richness of its conclusion, draped about your shoulders? It fucking stinks. Not of death exactly, something more dreadful than that. Life not lived. I don't know.

So out I go, knowing there's nothing for me there, only young women, who I know, in spite of what I read from their appearance, are human beings like me and have inner lives that roll like a threadbare carpet into painful pasts and uncertain futures. 'Where is this rehearsal space?' Rehearsal space. Life is not a rehearsal space, I say to myself as a postman whose accent drags me into the present charmingly bothers me for a photo, not for him like, for his missus. And I sort of want him to love me. The South London streets seem like a set.

His realness an anomaly. The tannery now an advertising agency called Pink Squid which on entering seems like an advert for itself. I mean literally no one was working, they were hanging out like people in, well, an advert for a youth-oriented brand, a Coke commercial maybe, having uncomplicated fun, playing foosball, on a game console – where is the money coming from and where is the money going? The postman doesn't know how to work his phone which is an iPhone from about five years ago so might as well be some artefact from the tannery. We do a photo, holding the phone backwards like in ancient history, not looking at the screen. For his missus. He's a postman so I ask where the rehearsal space is and he knows. It used to be a school, of course. Whither the kiddies now? Hmm? Ask not for whom the playtime bell tolls, it tolls for thee.

I think about climbing the wall at the back of the school to grab a bit of life back but instead go through a proper portal. When I was younger, when I was a junkie, a self-conscious and fragile pirate, I'd've been up and over in an instant and into that former playground. These days though I have a cereal bowl and a spoon. In a blue carrier bag I got from the ad agency. In I go to the rehearsal space to meet the theatre people. You can't tell this used to be a Victorian school with the lash of the cane and the gruel; it's so flooded with light and there's some sort of an exhibition on in the sky-lit foyer but I don't look at it. I march past the first reception because there is a notice on it which says 'REHEARSAL SPACE RECEPTION ON THE RIGHT'. I pause and pick it up and show it to the person behind the desk, I suppose because the sign seemed a bit shouty and I wanted to be directed to the appropriate desk quietly.

I barely have time to ask for Ian Rickson at the theatre people desk (no sign of Victorian schoolmasters, or even Maggie Thatcher-times teachers – ghosts, all beleaguered. In fact this is no longer a school at all, even on the phantom plane, it has been exorcised. And I wonder about some future hybrid me wandering a century down this fast-moving road, musing half sentimentally about the days when this used to be a minimalist rehearsal space – 'far as the eye could see') when Ian appears behind me, dressed like a summery person, even though this is pretty much autumn, a definite chill, and this morning I almost wore leather trousers. I couldn't, I didn't have the right shoes – they were in the car that I, saint that I am, surrendered to The Mother.

Ian directed *Jerusalem* and a bunch of other things with movie stars in them. He's kind to me but I've not known him long. In I go to the actual room I've been heading to and it's all vast and the floor is taped to resemble the stage that the play that Ian is rehearsing will eventually be performed on. So it's like another room has been murdered in this one, furniture an' all, and the police have taped round the outline of the numerous inanimate victims. There are a few people here, actors and theatre people – young though, not old like theatre. One is a friendly Irish man who has seen me do stand-up a few days previously and he's keen and kind. The other is a woman, she is young but has a soft, taut, maternal normalness that I still struggle not to grab at with my greedy mind. 'She's a human', I tell me, but me already knows. It's the humanness that me likes. It's not an objectification that is devoid of humanity; it is the appropriation of Woman A's physical traits to my own stifled agenda. Sometimes I feel like Hannibal Lecter when he's brought out on that trolley to help with a murder (that I think he was actually involved in devising, the fucker), I am strapped to a gurney and pale. I look out from my eyes into Woman A's eyes. The things I want are elemental. Warmth, softness, light. I have to put the cereal bowl down somewhere. It is in the blue bag and I am not the man in the cab or the man at home or the man in the ad agency. I am this man. In comes Zoë Wanamaker. I like her name. I like the late alphabet fusion – 'ZW'. I like her spritely hair. I like actresses and their bridled hysteria.

All the other people melt off and me and Zoë and Ian crunch carrot batons round a table that is playing the part of another table in another world.

We do the bit at the beginning, the small talk bit. I focus heavily on the carrots during this period because, like everyone in the world, I've never liked the beginning bit, the small talk. My mate Matt told me a few days ago that raw carrots kill gastric parasites so I just imagine the carotene apocalypse raining down on them while I half listen and half regret coming because I know I'll have to speak soon and knowing me I'll probably overdo it. Those little parasites won't know what's hit 'em. They'll be in there, doing what? Maybe building what they call a civilization, I don't see them as evil, I sort of think they might be nice. Matt says I probably got them in India and that's why I fart so much, but I don't mind farting. In fact I like it. I think of these parasites as my inner allies and feel a bit bad about bombing them out of existence with chemo-organic warfare.

Okay, my turn now. Zoë W has said something about seeing a Coke can whilst in the deepest backwaters of Rangoon and Ian is analysing deftly the clever use of African American stars and models and the odd, jarring proximity to sugarcane and slavery. Real me wants to say some dumb stuff now – silly, glib, naughty stuff about race and consumerism – but he mustn't. So instead I make some pretty good points about how a hundred years ago seeing a Coke can anywhere would've been weird and that we are all tribal people waking from the womb into a world of ersatz ad agencies and used-to-be schools (is that a Madonna song? No that's 'Playground', close enough) and that Osho says, 'Society is just a clearing in the forest', and I like that. A clearing in the forest. Nature, both inner and outer awaits a cessation and she will flood us anew with thorny green wonder. And my mind too, just a clearing in the forest, language structures and philosophical structures all heaped up high but built from nothing, like that clear plastic scaffold the Doozers in *Fraggle Rock* used to build.

Out we go for a fag in the playground and we move from small talk into actually discussing the Pinter play that we might do. *The Birthday Party*, it's called. Zoë W is very gentle and that is what I like. I can't take the hard edges of this world, this world I still can't fully commit to, after forty-one years and with a baby on the way. Luckily there is a wind chime tinkling away in a tangled melody, just behind me, I think in some sort of gestural vegetable garden. And I know and you know that dancing sound and dancing light, in myth at least, are signs of the presence of a higher thing. And if there are no signs? If there are no higher things? Then why should we continue with our meetings and our traffic jams and our parasites? If these things signify nothing and are just fully automated emblems of only themselves what is the point of theatre and poems or schools and advertising agencies? There is no point. But I know and you know (don't you?) that there is beneath the shash of thought and the wrought ascent and bilious plunge of feeling, some code of which the Sufis sung. Christ was, even if not the Son of God, surely not a blithering idiot, coming up with notions while picking at his nails. Whether you believe that Mohammed, peace be upon him, was the last prophet or not, there are evident truths in the prophecy that can scarcely be dismissed as babble.

Homeward I go, all crunched up on carrots, arm in arm with Wanamaker. Ambling up small streets, scattered with beauties and flanked by high-vis centurions, hollering in hard hats from the plinths they are constructing, I feel liberated. The woman knows how to play and how to be in the moment and what fucking relief there is in that. Every time I choked down a lungful of livid plastic crack, or swallowed the tail of the slick brown dragon it was with the prayer that they would deliver me unto the moment. And here I am in it.

She is being playfully maternal and I like it. Eventually though, chivalry asserts and I pop her in a hackney carriage and the loneliness that was one step ahead winds me almost as the cab door closes. The world gawps open like an old wound with new vigour and I am on three per cent battery life and not just on my phone. My wallet is in the car. I am alone. Like I used to be alone. On The Cut in Waterloo, one of those streets where old and new vie in ancient warfare and you can see the old tracks of who you used to be and who we used to be. And hooded people glide by and I jab at the screen, guiltily for an Uber as black cab drivers 'Oi, oi!' me. I like looking at the Uber screen as the potential cabs swarm like parasites round the pulsating blue dot. My driver's face appears on screen, not quite smiling. How many lit-up cabs will pass with their 'Oi, oi Russell's'? It's like a parade. The Uber cancels on me. My phone's now at one per cent. I start to sense I am abandoned. The phone dies and it's 1999 all over again. I lived round here then. Above a Barclays bank with Mark and Andy. No phone, no money. I feel like a Disney character, like I belong to a make-believe world. It's only a simulation, a drill, because of course I am not signing on. I am not living on benefits and drug-addicted. But I am still him, even if his life has changed, the essential self refracts now through a new prism, the new external coordinates, personal and social, remind me. I am famous, he was not. The Shard hadn't been built then, yet now it tears the sky in jagged certainty, unfinished. I was in there once and it was like a Ridley Scott film: bleak membrane drum-skin tight above the anxious city. I am soon to be a father and I don't take drugs and I am not penniless, I am penniful, if anything.

I walk along a market street, after the market has mostly departed and look for a joint to recharge my phone and think that it's like scoring. Like scoring power. There is a place called Cubana, as you might expect it is a Cuban-themed bar. Sugary cocktails, Che's face and a Kalashnikov stencilled on a wall, and the staff seem mostly

> 'In this cab I do not feel like the saint I want to be, I do not feel like a prophet or even a priest. I feel like ET or someone left behind. I feel homeless, landless.'

Spanish and it's hard to locate what the intention is of an ironic communist revolutionary bar in London in 2016 because of the palpable need for real change, the need for sincerity, the need for the opposite of an ironic Cuban revolution-themed bar, whatever that is. No one there has an iPhone 6s charger, they're a Samsung crowd, and sadly I discover that I am not famous in that particular room so shuffle onward in the role of a bloke who needs a charger, not an elevated version of me. I land eventually at a bookshop cafe built on good intentions a few hundred yards down and charge my phone there. 'Everyone does,' says Abigail at the till, 'we're so near Waterloo station.' The bookshop is called Travelling Through. I sit a while upon the floor and watch the green bar rise like the thermometer on an unwatched telethon until I am powerful enough to leave. By now I've organized a cab and the fleeting simulation of normal life, or life without means, has ended and ten minutes was enough to leave me doubled over inside. In the cab leaving London I am angry. I feel like I lost something there and the traffic is heavy and pointless. I stare out of the window waiting for something to make sense. I've lived all over London so its streets teem with a deep geology of agonized nostalgia. I see me sixteen and zipping round the Tube map like Puck, like I'd invented drugs, tripping the light fandango. I see me nineteen, downing pints of cider and acting my little socks off at drama school. I see me twenty, getting nicked and knowing it was going to be okay, that it was all content, that something would lift me above these streets and plonk me down on top and here I am seething in the back of a cab, having been all sorts of people, all sorts of famous, all sorts of glamorous, sensing it's all over. The way I sensed drugs were over.

In this cab I do not feel like the saint I want to be. I do not feel like a prophet or even a priest. I feel like ET or someone left behind. I feel homeless, landless. My friend Amie calls. Amie, an intravenous heroin user since her early teens, has suffered abuse that chokes me to recount. She has been a sex worker for most of her life and has spent too much time in prison. 'You sound fucking dreadful,' she says. I say I am fine, I can't take another bit of bullshit though. I'm all bullshitted out. She laughs at this and talks about herself, her trip to the National Theatre to watch *The Seagull*, her relationship with her ongoing dream to become an actor. She at some point remarks upon the tenacity of addicts like me. We keep trying. We don't kill ourselves. An addict friend of mine said the day before, 'A theist is a person who has seen through the material and mechanical world and doesn't commit suicide'. I like this quote. To see that it is all bullshit and not to clock off, that requires faith. Only faith will do. Only faith. Even if you're double certain that there is nothing but space and dumb molecules out there, clattering about into symphonic and faraway futures, if you believe that's all there is and don't check out, you are hardcore. You must really love football or fucking or money or something and be okay with those things being only what they explicitly are, without implicit power, with no unravelling flag blowing behind them in limitless wind, back to before some unknowable moment of creation when this universe's heart first began to beat. Oddly, it is Amie who performs my restoration after the terror of the ordinary had undone me. Her easy understanding of the resident rage that takes me hostage, when tripped over by nostalgia, when strewn on terrible and familiar streets, of how hard it is to carry on connecting when your battery runs out. When I get home, I see that it's all real. I do indeed have a pregnant girlfriend. She is pleased to see me, astonished as I am, that I have returned home with a cereal bowl.

Step 6 Exercises: Well that's revealed a lot of fucked up patterns. Do you want to stop it? Seriously?

During Steps 4 and 5 we learned a lot about ourselves. What we had taken to be random external events, or particularly poor fortune, now begins to look like a drama in which we participate. Of course there is such a thing as 'bad luck' and 'people being dicks', perhaps there always will be, but by doing our inventory we can see just how our problematic attitudes, thoughts and behaviour have made our lives much harder. List your problematic attitudes/thoughts/behaviour patterns, these are commonly known as 'defects'. We can use the list from the Step 4, fourth column, Faults section.

With each defect we identify ask:

- Why do I do this? How does it help me? (What do I want, or want to avoid?)
- If I do not change, what will happen?
- If I am willing to change, how could my life improve?
- Do I want this defect removed? Am I ready to let go?
- If the answer is 'no', ask yourself: how is my life unmanageable due to my powerlessness to change this attitude/thought/ behaviour pattern?

Defective behaviours often seem to be of benefit. They are strategies that seem to have worked even if at an undiagnosed but painful spiritual cost.

For example, my promiscuity prevented me from noticing that I felt lonely, weak, worthless and unattractive. My anxiety and fretting, I tell myself, are a kind of alertness. I have through inventorying and sharing come to see the true cost of these defective behaviours and am now ready for them 'to be removed'.

The truth is defective behaviours lead to pain. We must be willing to let go of them all. Entirely.

Ask yourself:

- Am I willing to let go of my egocentric, self-centred world view?
- Am I willing to tear up my plan?
- Am I willing to stop blaming others? To let go of resentment?
- Am I willing to use this program as the new plan for my life?
- Am I willing to accept that there are more powerful forces than me in the universe and that in this context my motives and notions are ridiculous?

I accept this all seems quite evangelical. If you bridle at this it's likely that on some level you think, 'I want to change, but not that much', or, 'I'd like to be a bit better but I like some of my negative attributes and materialistic, individualistic conditioning, it helps me to be a good consumer'. This is a popular perspective. Again, those of us who find this world a little hard to bear must query what our discomfort is telling us. Sometimes the road is long but eventually, once called, we must walk it.

Remember, vitally, we work this program one day at a time. It is this manageable time frame that makes many of the absolutes that preclude egocentric conditioning conceivable. I am still astonished by my tendency to adorn and adore the bars of my cage. Only through this program have I known freedom.

7

Are you willing to live in a new way that's not all about you and your previous, fucked up stuff? You have to.

Step 7: We humbly asked Him to remove our shortcomings.

Step 7 is about humility, it is about accepting the limits of our model of reality. It is about 'accepting what we are and embracing what we could become'.

Foucault would tell you, if he were here and you could get him to cooperate, that the very notion of an inner connection to a divine being is a social and linguistic construct that we need to abandon, and that we invent ourselves rather than discovering ourselves. I disagree with Michel here, mostly on the basis of my personal experience with distinct and seemingly transcendent aspects of 'my own' consciousness, and not only while off my nut on drugs. I accept that there are limitations to the capacity of this book but I invite you, implore you even, to consider that your model of reality, if painful, is in need of improvement, and the humility and faith that are components of this 'way' will set you free.

A modern view of prayer could be 'an earnest attempt to commune with the aspect of your consciousness that is untainted by learned thought patterns or fluctuations caused by biochemical impulse'. Can we tend towards that? The experience of jealousy, the experience of envy or rage. Can we reach through the fear to the crucible of Self, which is experiencing sensation and thought and ask that we transcend our baser wants? We know, don't we, that little is achieved through constant self-centredness? We know too that it is objectively ridiculous to obsess about our own wants and desires. Humility is the acknowledgement of our relative insignificance – our insignificance when compared to the infinite, or even all the other people currently alive. Not that we are without value, no, we are infinitely valuable in so much as we are part of the infinite. Our personal drives and wants though are either automated biological impulses or neurotic ticks and quirks that we have unconsciously subscribed to. If I believe that I can only be happy if I am in a particular relationship, and the other person doesn't seem to be interested or doesn't conform to the way I believe they should behave, it is, in the scheme of things, unimportant. And if I allow my feelings about the situation to bleed into all other areas of my life, work, child-rearing and friendships, this is an indication that I am being self-centred and have lost my humility. There is sadness in the world, there is disappointment. All that is in the material world will transpire; the sun itself, let alone our planet, will one day implode and when it does it will be a day like this one, a moment, a time, if time exists on a galactic level, like this one. So from that perspective my romantic concerns are quite minor. My esteem then ought to be derived from the fact that I am part of this great play, and if I can cleanse myself of acquired mental habits and redundant or detrimental biological drives, I can live in the service of a positive and creative force.

The rather Christian-sounding prayer for Step 7, given that the program was constructed in the USA in the thirties, is unsurprisingly in the appropriate vernacular and reads:

> 'My Creator,
> I am now willing that You should have all of me, good and bad.
> I now pray that you remove every single defect of character that
>   stands between me and my usefulness to You and my fellows.
> Grant me strength as I go out from here to do Your bidding.'

'My Creator' is relatively modern; at least it isn't gender specific or a loaded word like 'Master'. The term 'My Creator' can easily apply to whatever great mystery you conceive of that is driving evolution and universal expansion.

I am now willing that You should have all of me, good and bad.

Of course, I slip up on a daily basis, mid-interaction I think, "hang on, I'm being totally selfish here", but I only have this awareness because I work this program. I have a template.'

Here the willingness is key, we are no longer saying, 'This is just the way I am' or 'What's wrong with being self-centred?' Having reviewed our inventory, we have decided we want to eliminate our defective characteristics, our patterns that generated personal and general misery. We acknowledge here that we have positive attributes, that we are capable of kindness and love: we are not total shitbags. I like the way this prayer suggests a higher proprietor, a surrender to a higher way. The Hindu deity Ganesh is known as 'the remover of obstacles'. I often envisage my jealousy or self-righteousness being removed by this Ganesh force to allow the clear and undiminished light to radiate. The word Islam of course means 'surrender'; in this context we surrender our selfish former habits in faith that beyond them, with the channel clear, a Higher Power will transmit.

I now pray that you remove every single defect of character that stands between me and my usefulness to You and my fellows.

This is the explicit expression of a higher goal. We no longer operate on the *mundial* level of self-fulfilment like cattle. We pledge to be useful. It is utilitarianism that we are guided by. We prepare ourselves for service. Instead of my only goal in life being the fulfilment of my own picayune needs, I make myself available to a higher purpose. To this force, as I conceive it and experience it, and practically other people. How can I be useful to other people?

Now there's a concept in 2017: 'help others'. Do something that is not for you, maybe not even for someone you know. Being kind to my girlfriend is like cleaning my teeth or flushing the toilet: it's good that I do it but if I don't I will suffer. My partnership is the relationship that I tangibly live in. If I start being kind to people I don't know, from whom I cannot derive benefit, now that's advanced. And to take it to black belt levels, try doing kind things and then not telling anybody about it. Maybe in the next life!

Grant me strength as I go out from here to do Your bidding.

Here the prayer reveals its petition, we want strength, but only so we can be useful, not so that we can win *The X Factor* or run a juice bar, unless we are certain that this is what the Higher Power wants for us. A good way to find out the will of your Higher Power is to ask someone else, someone you trust, who has a program. When I say this prayer, at the 'go out from here', I imagine 'here' to be my heart, and that I will try to live my life and do my work from my heart. Step 7 is a powerful step and one I work continuously. Of course, I slip up on a daily basis, mid-interaction I think, 'Hang on, I'm being totally selfish here', but I only have this awareness because I work this program, I have a template. And because I have worked Step 6, I am willing to change, I have admitted that selfishness and lust do not work for me. So if I find myself lying to get what I want or staring at someone as if they had no purpose in this world but to give me pleasure and escape, I can see that I am now off track. The prayer is an agreement with the Self that you would like to be. With this program, at any time you find yourself going off track, moving away from the person you would like to be, the person you were intended to be before malevolent thinking and behaviour and habits took hold, you can use this formula to guide you home.

When I say the Step 7 prayer I call to mind what I know of evolutionary theory, the unknowable beauty of the universe's inception, the slow dawning of our planet, the birth of chemistry and biology, the mysterious forces that either drive, facilitate or allow this process, the emergence of cellular life, its crescendo over millions of years to self-conscious life – life that is capable of contemplating its own creation. I consider this when I say 'My Creator'. I also consider the part of my own being that has sat in witness to the events of my life so far. The part of me that has observed the chaos and yearning somehow unimpaired, 'My Creator'. The rest of the prayer, even if prayer to you is no more than 'having a word' with yourself, is a fine appeal to offer.

I am now willing that You should have all of me, good and bad.

I like the acknowledgement of the good and bad. I like the humility of placing my life in a context that exceeds the pursuit of my own petty, trivial desires. As Adam Curtis says, 'We have been taught that freedom is the freedom to pursue our petty, trivial desires. Real freedom is freedom from our petty, trivial desires.' I sense there is true freedom here, even if I am afraid.

When at Amma's ashram in Kerala, southern India a swami said to me, 'The world has nothing else to give you now, Russell. It can only take from you', I felt a chill. Like 'the game is up'. He was right. After he said that I continued to try to use the world to my advantage – prestige, power, appearances – all to no avail, always left with an anxious deficit in my belly. I hardly need tell you that I still err daily, but now at least I have sound ideals towards which I am willing to aim. What use am I to this all-encompassing entity or the Earth's people if I am rife with defects? Little.

The second part of this beautiful 'consciousness hack' asks that we be useful to God and our fellows. A useful tool for me each day then this prayer, in possession as I am of a mind that reverts to selfish aims. If I think 'how can I be useful to the man serving me coffee' or to any and

None of us can adequately control the meteorology of other people: they're nice, they're nasty, they come, they go. We have no choice but to address, alter and amend the inner coordinate.'

each of the people I encounter over a day, my experience of reality is enhanced. Finally:

Grant me strength as I go out from here to do Your bidding.

I always envisage 'going out' from my heart, lovingly, kindly and then witness if the vow can withstand London traffic. In short be willing to be a different person, rather than Russell MK1, who ultimately would sacrifice anything to see his needs fulfilled.

Humility then is to acknowledge one's relative insignificance. Not worthlessness, we are valuable but through our connection to the whole, not the mental and material acquisitions achieved through the agency of ego.

When you're recognizable, privacy becomes a commodity. I have escaped from the glamour and nausea I sought to live in comfortable domesticity. On the river at night I am free on glistening silence and I see my girlfriend in the darkness as she is, an independent entity that shares life with me. In the day, the shameful day, the river is Christmas busy. The river has locks. Locks are a feat of engineering, managing the flow of water, preventing flood but subtler forces of nature escape their punctuation. I am shy and bob about in a rowboat, making small talk across the bows and big judgements in my swollen mind. In the ordinary moment the melodrama surges and plunges, the thoughts torrential and tyrannical. Worrying and judging, ever protecting the raw, bare boy, who's in there parentless, unbounded.

So sloshing about in the lock with wet ropes and maritime incompetence we are vulnerable to a sudden paparazzi. Laura is pregnant and exposed. Adjacent to the river, post lock, there is some kind of fun-run happening and in the midst of this the pap snaps further. Laura, though far from a 'hit him Wayne' type girlfriend, in her pregnant and vulnerable state expresses irritation and we razz each other up into action. Meaning I pootle over to the riverbank, wade out, join the 'fun-run', at a jog and not in the fun spirit that the organizers intended, I mean I'm fuming. As far as I'm concerned it's a rage run. I'm careful to conserve breath because I'm keen not to waddle up to the pudgy pap all wheezy as I know deep down that I'm on the brink of my patented and all too frequent (even if there has only been a handful) Ray Winstone confrontation tone.

Slowing down I place an angry hand on his shoulder like an avid *Daily Mail* reader citizen's-arresting a Maddy suspect. 'Get any good shots mate?' I purr menacingly.

This overt and theatrical rendering of our contemporary working-class masculinity an attempt to parent the raw, bare boy in the lock. A program is being worked, an unconscious program. We do not choose between program and no program, we choose between a conscious program and the unconscious program that operates us by default.

By working through my Step 4, the 'thorough and fearless inventory' and the subsequent 'fear inventory'; a more specific itinerary of the fears that underscore my defective actions, I have identified components of the code that make up my unconscious default program. That 1) I am afraid to die, 2) I am afraid that I can't take care of myself and 3) I am afraid that I cannot trust anyone.

In this scenario core fear number 2 is at work: I am afraid that I cannot take care of myself therefore I have to counter that belief with a contrary action, in this case acting all tough when a more sensible course of action would obviously have been to ignore the provocation. So the external stimulant of the threatening pap engages in a live connection with my inner fear that I can't take care of myself and in this moment I have no strategy to override this inner and outer negative circuit. I have lost myself. None of us can adequately control the meteorology of other people: they're nice, they're nasty, they come, they go. We have no choice but to address, alter and amend the inner coordinate if we want to have a different model of reality, if we want to have more choices.

Hot and bothered I say to the pap, 'Delete the photos'. My unstated plan is to get his camera and lob it in the river, even though it is strapped onto him like Rambo's rifle. I settle for snatching his spectacles to barter for the film, or whatever passes for film in the post-digital world.

At this point my connection to the source is gone, I am not consciously trying to be a good man. On the contrary, I am a connoisseur of my own malevolent feelings, relishing like a vampire my cold contempt of the porcine voyeur. When some of the jaunty, passing fun-runners pause to ask me for a selfie, I make much of obliging like some garrulous John Candy character, all hugs and smiles, to emphasize to ol' porky that the Ray Winstone act is just one role in my locker (stocker and two smoking barrels).

It is extremely important that you recognize that the significant activity here took place in the realm of thought. My own negative programming meant the external event was coloured, filtered, inflected in a manner that made negative outcomes inevitable. What this program can do is give you another option. The nature of the challenges vary but the number of inner coordinates is limited, perhaps in the same way that most human beings have the same basic organic set-up: we all have hearts and kidneys and lungs. My sense is that our inner faculties, our emotional palate, are similarly comparable. Whether you're a gnarled and boisterous apprentice mechanic or a Cambridge don, solving conundrums from your high-tech wheelchair, there is in most cases a comparable inner world. If not a basic binary, a universal pantheon of inner deities and demons which, in our race to total rationalism, we have unwisely discarded. The Greeks knew these gods dwelt not on Olympus but upon the summits, crags and slopes within. This inner realm interfaces with external phenomena for good or for ill. This program, like all mythology, is a methodology for management.

On this day I yielded my program to the program that abides when I am not present. After a bit of snarling and handbaggery I left the pap sans specs and shot off back to Laura. Already the fugue is clearing. Already I am beginning to see – perhaps because I have acquired a pair of glasses, that my conduct was imprudent. 'I think I've just been stupid, Laura,' I say wading back into the boat.

The pap calls the police. The police know who I am and where I live. This whole scenario is a product of fame and the personality that drove me to seek it.

I was out but Laura was at home with my in-laws who have already had to roll back fathomless logic to accept me into their hearts so when the ol' 5.0 comes a-knocking at the door it must be hard for them to see me as reformed Russell, man of peace, as opposed to Russell, the junkie, sex addict, prank phone-calling, trouble-making narcissist. Of course I'm both of these characters and the reality I manifest is hugely improved by adherence to this discipline.

If we choose to live in a materialistic perception of this happenstance I get tangled in the weeds of 'How come that pap can steal and profit from my image but I can't take his specs?' Or 'How come the police even know where I live?' I have no choice but to see the event as a symbol in my personal myth, to look for the lessons that it is trying to suggest to me. To do this I need some basic principles, gratitude and acceptance.

I am grateful for my life where I get to show off for a living, and as a consequence of this I will occasionally be photographed. Now if I were you, reading this, determined not to change my *Weltanschauung* ('world view' in German), I'd go, 'That's easy for you to say, you're loaded and you're on a rowboat on the Thames with yer luvverly bird of course you can accept a modicum of inconvenience.' Well here is my riposte: 'If you determine your life by external data, there will always be something to complain about. There will always be some facet of reality that is not going as you would like it to. There is always more to be consumed, people more rich and famous than you. To be clear, unless I'm much mistaken you're not reading this in a ditch in the slums of Kibera with the barrel of a gun in your mouth while a rabid warlord bums you for his amusement are you?' And yet that horrific scenario (other than having to read this book while it happens) is reality for some people. In fact half of humanity live in conditions of galling poverty so any of us that have swerved that nightmare would do well to not spend our leisure time bemoaning the fact that we are not laid out on a yacht with a Kardashian slurping away at our privates because, the sages are right, the material world is an illusion and its treasures all too temporal.

That doesn't mean you have to live as a monk, although that is one way out of it, it just means you can never quench your spiritual craving through material means. Gratitude for where you are and what you have is one important coordinate for retuning our consciousness. Similarly acceptance. We are where we are supposed to be. From this position we can grow, with inner resistance comes tumult. I would never propose that you ought to accept injustice or be anything other than all that you can possibly be. This step enables us through humble petition to a Higher Self, to experience deep peace and a power that is present and waiting to be unlocked. This is not a moral or economic argument. This is a system for managing your inner life so that you can deal with reality.

We crave connection, but so much of the time we are not alive, neutralized. Who are you when you're listening to the radio in traffic? You are not you, you are on standby. Mostly we are free-floating and disengaged, lost in the spectacle. When I fixate on the object of my addiction in any given moment, it is because I believe it will give me relief from disconnection. Even if it will ultimately make things worse, I will feel the connection. This is why addicts relapse even though they have strong evidence that the action will not be successful. Once they are in the traumatized, cut-off state they revert to the only plan they know to ameliorate the feeling. Through humility this step bypasses our erroneous and illusory methods for temporary self-salvation and connects us to the truth we have always sought: we are, in fact, connected.

Step 7 Exercises: Are you willing to live in a new way that's not all about you and your previous, fucked up stuff? You have to.

Recovery, this way of life upon which I hope you embark, comprises only guidance and power. A friend of mine says 'Satellite navigation system plus fuel'. With the removal of defects, I need to ask to commune with the Supreme Truth, the Unified Field, God, as I understand God, for a new vision. Then I need to ask for the strength to put this into practice. The steps that follow provide the framework for this transformation.

Having 'become ready' to change our shady behaviour and thinking in the previous step, we make a decision that seems oddly incremental, we 'ask for them to be removed'.

It is a common spiritual dictum that each flaw or 'sin' contains within it an attribute waiting to be realized. Early in my recovery with my first mentor I came up with a notion, based on the fourteen character defects as he showed them to me, that (even if I do say it myself) perspicaciously foreshadowed this idea.

Here are the defects as I then understood them, although now, as you have seen, I use a more exhaustive list.

Pride, Self-pity, Self-centredness, Selfishness, Intolerance, Impatience, Jealousy, Envy, Lust, Sloth, Greed, Gluttony, Arrogance, Dishonesty.

When 'humbly' asking for our defects to be removed (by God!!) consider what attribute would most usefully replace them.

- Self-pity – compassion for others
- Selfishness – kindness
- Self-centredness – empathy

- Intolerance, Dishonesty and Impatience are obvious –
  their opposites
- Lust – love
- Greed – generosity
- Gluttony – mindfulness
- Sloth – diligence
- Arrogance – humility
- Envy – gratitude
- Jealousy – acceptance
- Pride – grace

These, like much of this book, are simply a guide to a different way of thinking. When I am navigated into loving attitudes my life is a joy to inhabit. Which surely is partly the point.

Humility is our acknowledgement of our relative insignificance. We are valuable as part of the whole and we have a right to love and be loved but we can afford to surrender the egoic authorship that has got us into this pickle.

If you are an atheist or agnostic and the idea of asking God to remove defects is a bit mental but you do want to change, this is how I'd do it.

I'd say this out loud:

'I don't know if there is a supreme being out there in the limitless cosmos, in fact, I don't think there is. I do know that my thinking is limited as it takes place within the context of my own knowledge, which is bounded on all sides by ignorance. I am open to the possibility that beneath my thoughts, my feelings, the invisible field that holds together my material being are other forces that are likely beyond human comprehension and the dualistic models, and space/time framework through which we understand reality. Within this limitlessness all is possible. I as a limited entity petition with

my awakening, personal consciousness that which is beyond limits and contains within it all creativity, all joy, all beauty and I ask that my life and consciousness can be used as a vessel for these positive powers.'

Then if you're super ironic and self-aware, say 'Amen'. What harm can it do?

You may not immediately become perfect. None of us will – whether we believe in a supernatural, causeless authority or not – but I predict you and your relationship with external and internal phenomena will improve.

Ask yourself:

- What do I want to change?
- Am I going to change it?
- Do I commit to change?

8

Prepare to apologize to everyone for everything affected by your being so fucked up.

Step 8: We made a list of all persons we had harmed, and became willing to make amends to them all.

Having altered my understanding of a Higher Power (through the first three steps) and of myself (through 4, 5, 6 and 7), my attention was turned to the damage I had done to others. There were a lot of people that had been harmed by my behaviour. One of the great challenges everyone faces with Step 8 is distinguishing it from Step 9. Step 9 is about making amends. Step 8 is about making a list and becoming willing. We don't reflect or project on what making the amends might be like, or whether or not we want to make them while compiling the list. If you do that it disrupts the process. The people that structured this program were masterful. They understood that if you envisaged making the amends while making the list, you would omit people from the list; it is a nimble piece of construction and we must abide by it. The second great challenge I found was one of forgiveness. Becoming willing to 'make amends to people I had harmed' meant that in many cases I had to forgive any harms I believed they'd done to me.

This is where we must understand what amends are for and what the word really means. Amend means 'to change or improve'. While restitution, recompense or restoration is part of this process the key is change. We do not want to be the same people anymore; we have acknowledged our way wasn't working. We have come to believe that we can be different; we've decided to become teachable. We've had a good thorough look at ourselves; we've told someone else about it. We've become willing to get rid of the negative traits identified and we've asked, humbly, for them to be removed. So we want to change. It is hard to start anew if your past is littered with damage and your conscience cluttered with guilt and shame. What kind of a self-help book would this be if I overlooked the opportunity to tell you that 'guilt is about what you've done' and 'shame is about who you are'?

'These were furious diatribes of undiluted rage. Reading them out before the group of other sex addicts sparked in me such volatile and uncontrollable rage that I spun around, picked up the chair I'd previously been sitting on and smashed it on the wall.'

Guilt and shame tether us to old ways of seeing and being. They are very difficult codes to rewrite. Steps 8 and 9 are integral to the process of shifting our perception of who we are. I'll give you some of my experience around this. In my Step 4, which you are now beginning to understand is vital for progression and for the execution of all subsequent steps, I had a good many resentments against myself. Some were for things like 'not being good enough at football' or 'not having a good enough body' but others were for harms I had done to other people, like 'myself for cheating on Elia', a girlfriend I was with for a few years when I was in my early twenties, or 'myself for not being present the third time my mum got cancer'. With these resentments I had to look exclusively at my own behaviour. What this means is I had to get over my previous perspective on these events. It is unhelpful to justify your own behaviour when making this list – to say 'Well, Elia should've had more sex with me' or 'I was on drugs, I didn't know what I was doing'. Thinking of this kind prevents growth because I am still validating the behaviour through continued justification. I look only at what I did: I cheated on Elia. With one of her friends. I subjected her to much selfishness, I used her.

With the resentment involving my mother, it's no use saying 'It's not my fault she got ill' or 'I was only a kid' or 'It's not my job to look after her' or 'I hated my stepdad'. These beliefs, these codes, are all impediments to improvement. There are even more complex resentments to consider, my dad and stepdad, two men who I believed had done me great wrong. When I was in a treatment centre for sexual addiction in my late twenties one of the exercises was to write a letter to them, that blessedly remains unsent, letting them know what I thought of them. In both cases these were furious diatribes of undiluted rage. Reading them out before the group of other sex addicts sparked in me such volatile and uncontrollable rage that I spun around, picked up the chair I'd previously been sitting on and smashed it on the wall. This led to me almost being sectioned in a Philadelphia mental institution, which on the basis of my brief visit, would not have been a cool place to be impounded. I felt that my stepdad despised me, that he made no effort to father me. There were a few physical altercations when I got older. Sufficient material for me to remain resentful. But what's the point in that? Why would I want to hold on to an emotion that hurts me, turning my body and spirit into a vessel for 'justifiable' pain?

This program helps me to change my perspective when what I would do unabetted is justify my perspective staying the same – 'If you do what you've always done, you'll get what you've always got'. If you want change, you have to change. You have to make amends. This in the case of my stepdad meant two things, the first being forgiveness. This is pretty easy when you get into it. Here's how: he is just a human being like me. He is not perfect, like me. It is not my job to adjudicate the world's people and supply them with a template for how they should be. In fact it's none of my business. There is only one human being I'm in control of and that is me, and that is where the effort must be concentrated. Forgiveness is a powerful spiritual tool, without it we are damned as individuals and as a people. Forgiveness means letting go. It means being willing to accept that we are all mortals flawed and suffering, imperfectly made and trying our best. That sometimes there is a collision of instinct. He was trying to live his life, have a relationship with my mother, work nights in a job he didn't like and support another man's son. He was doing his best. Am

I unwilling to forgive? Am I determined that the world must be as I decree? Do I see a future in that way of thinking, especially when it's done nothing but bring me pain so far? What am I holding on to? What is gained by withholding forgiveness, for ruminating on a concluded event, by holding on to bygone pain and wishing ill upon a man just like me? Nothing.

Looking at my own life it is clear how greatly I have erred. How can I expect forgiveness if I am unwilling to forgive? What of the few incidents in my childhood where I was transgressed against sexually? Do I have to ransack those events mentally, looking for novel ways to blame myself? Of course not, this is an opportunity though to amend my perception of those events and improve my life as a result. It is of course wrong that I was touched up by a man when I was seven years old and when looking at my part I am not seeking to minimize his responsibility. What I am doing is releasing myself from the pain I have been unconsciously carrying. So I don't have to say, like some awful eighties judge, that I was a terrible little flirt and brought it on myself, that would of course be nuts. What I can do is accept that this event happened, that it was not my fault, that it is over and it is not happening now and not to allow it to continue to block my path to mental and spiritual clarity. By forgiving the perpetrator, I release myself. I can revise the event. I can see it as something that gives me more compassion and understanding. I can let go of it. There is no benefit to establishing an imaginary judicial system in my own mind where I carry out punishments to people who have wronged me. By letting go of this long-held inner drama I become a little more liberated and useful. In essence it's bad that it happened but it's worse that I allow myself to be affected by it now. I cannot control the past but I can control the present through forgiveness.

I have heard beautiful tales of forgiveness and its eminence in the spiritual life is often testified to. I have heard of mothers forgiving their son's murderer, befriending the killer, learning to understand and love the person who has cost them so dearly, knowing that there is no freedom without forgiveness. In the prayer of Saint Francis he says, 'it is by forgiving that we are forgiven', and this means I suppose that there is a direct connection between the clemency we express and the world that we experience. That old school staple, the Lord's Prayer, says, 'Forgive us our trespasses as we forgive those who trespass against us'. Freedom has a clause: it is forgiveness. Or as Gandhi would have it, 'Be the change you want to see in the world'. If we want forgiveness, we must forgive.

Once I had forgiven my stepdad, I was able to look more clearly at my own actions. I was rude, dismissive and disruptive. I stole, I lied and I manipulated. These are harms. So when I make a list of people I have harmed, he must be on it. I must say I felt a kind of liberation having made this adjustment, a sense of freedom that came just from throwing off the yoke of my own tyrannizing perspective. It felt as if I'd advanced from the image I'd had of myself, life and circumstances as a boy to a liberating maturation, manhood. By maintaining a personal museum of resentments, we imprison ourselves within it.

There are limitless ways that we may have harmed people or damaged institutions through our behaviour. Not all of them will be found on our Step 4 inventory. It is important that we are able to discern where real harm has been done as opposed to projections of our own feelings of guilt and shame. It is important to undertake this process under guidance and with the support of a community to ensure that we are conducting it safely and prudently. The guiding principle being that we do not want to cause more harm.

I now recall that I owe a financial amends to MTV. When I was first given a job with them I was twenty-four years old and my addiction was in the ascendency. I was steadily graduating to pretty radical chemical dependency and working at MTV, based in Camden, London, was the perfect environment to incubate this condition. The building there – a jostling hub of glistening beauties, novelty desk toys, freebies, cool trainers and optimism – was right on the canal. The canal was continually patrolled by drug dealers. I skipped between these two worlds like Alice. I can't have been the only person who was using drugs there, obviously. I probably wasn't the only person there with a drug problem; it's just that I was able to make my drug problem an effective contagion, interfering with the lives of anyone who came into contact with it. I was, as I am now, quite an intense and energetic person, so I was able to cause a lot of bother in a short period of time.

When you are given a job as a presenter at MTV, they give you an account number for the London-based cab firm Addison Lee, ostensibly for use when you travel to and from work. In my case this would've meant a couple of journeys a week. But when that account code hit my unrefined, addict mind I instantly decided that I would never be using public transport again. Not only that, I would never knowingly not use the account if the possibility existed: pizzas, drugs, sex workers and (less troublingly) my mother were all freely ferried around using this service. It is a good example of how my mind works. If I am given an opportunity, in this case, the privilege of free travel to work, I will exploit it like the East India Trade Company plundering their colony. I had no inhibiting boundary or morality that could curb the use of those taxis. Only on one occasion, when someone else, my dear friend Andy Milligan, the producer who had first given me a job there, called from a Soho club asking if he could use the account did I momentarily discover a modicum of morality. 'This cab account is for professional use': I shudder at the memory. Andy made it onto my Step 8 list but MTV didn't. I was able to mentally justify my behaviour for over fourteen years: they're a huge corporation, they don't care, they're basically 'the man', I was doing what any self-respecting drug addict would do rinsing a good opportunity for all it was worth, I don't know how much money it was or even who I would pay it back to. None of these excuses are acceptable to me anymore. As I have indicated this program and its benefits have come slowly to me. I am much more at the remedial end of the scale. Now though, with fourteen and a half years clean and sober and the sense of rectitude that engenders, I have become willing to make amends to MTV. That means I'll have to find out who's the boss there now, call up and make an appointment, go in and tell them I'm an addict, part of my program is to make amends to people I have wronged and that I owe them an amends. But what I am describing there is Step 9, which is naturally what follows Step 8, and 'having made a list of all that we have harmed, and become willing to make amends to them all', this is where we now find ourselves. Step 8 is where we stop justifying our story. We stop clinging to the past. We recognize that if we want to go forward we will need to change. Part of that change is forgiveness and the willingness to look at our lives and the world differently. Ask yourself 'Do I really want to change or do I just want to justify staying the way that I am?'

Step 8 Exercises: Prepare to apologize to everyone for everything affected by your being so fucked up.

Go through your Step 4. Anybody, or any institution you have harmed, add to a list. Remember that list you wrote of everyone you encountered? Anyone on there that causes a wrench in your gut when you read their name ought to be on the list. Don't worry if you feel they also harmed you, it's not a quiz show or the US justice system – it's a technique to cleanse the consciousness. The fourth column, 'Wrongs' section will also be of particular use.

Then for each item, or more likely person on the list note (or if you want to take it up a gear use an index card) the name and:

- What you did that was harmful
- What you should have done instead
- Who suffered as a result, and how

Harm could be something obvious like 'I stole their bike', or less tangible like 'I robbed them of their peace of mind'.

Referring again to our Step 4 we use the seven areas of our lives that are 'affected', the third column, to discern what may have been affected in them.

The second question helps us discern what we could've done instead – sometimes the suffering caused was unavoidable, e.g.:

Stopping my dog savaging sheep (what am I going to do? Not hold him back? His irritation/suffering was necessary).

Leaving a bad relationship (I had to leave, I'd've gone crazy).

This list ought to be devoid of analysis and speculation. Ideally you should be able to clearly envisage the harm by reading the card.

Dave – I took his bike. I should not have taken his bike.

Not a bunch of speculation about Dave's inner drama surrounding the bike. The 12 Step program has among its many epithets 'Keep it simple' – knowing that we have a tendency to needlessly complicate stuff. This is important with this step.

Once you have completed the list and the above questions you have to ask yourself in each case:

● **Am I willing to make amends to this person?**

The purpose of this step is to free us from our attachment to old ways of thinking and grant us a new life. This willingness is an indicator of real change.

It clearly involves forgiveness, which can be hard to accept but is clearly a powerful tool in changing our perception of the past, our value as individuals and moving freely into the future.

9

Now apologize.
Unless that would
make things worse.

Step 9: We made direct amends to such people wherever possible, except when to do so would injure them or others.

Secretly, I always liked the look of this step. It's cinematic. It involves a quest. It has the drama of me moseying through the past, all full of potent Sergio Leone scored wisdom, offering squinting and self-righteous apologies to all the people I had hurt, rogue that I was. By the time I reached Step 9 I had been disabused of this shallow romanticism. Step 9 is a good example of the intersection of pragmatism and mysticism that this program demonstrates again and again. What's the point in spirituality if it doesn't make you feel better? If you don't feel better as a result of doing this program, there is no point doing it. You might as well carry on with whatever demented behaviour you were employing in the first place. It is practical because it is, on the surface, solely about action. You have 'made a list of all the people that you have harmed and become willing to make amends to them all'. Now you crack on and make those amends. This means researching and soul searching. Researching because you may for example, just off the top of my head, need to track down the head of accounts at MTV UK in the late nineties. It involves soul searching because of the caveat 'unless to do so would injure them or others'.

In my Step 8 there were instances where it was very difficult for me to 'become willing'. I talked you through the process of forgiveness that was required with my stepdad. I had to unpick all the wrongs I believed he'd done me to have a clear view of the wrongs I'd done him. Then I had to decide what form the amends would take. By the time I'd gotten round to forgiving him and becoming ready, he was no longer with my mum. He was no longer immediately accessible, which gave me a reason to avoid him. Also, I reasoned, he was always a quiet man, not given to discussing emotions and would

153

probably find this whole business bloody embarrassing. Neither of these rationalizations constitute justifiable inaction. While I was contemplating him and the process involved, one thought kept returning: in my autobiography *My Booky Wook*, I had laid into him with a total lack of restraint, with relish actually. I'd written only my side of the argument and gracelessly depicted him as a kind of Dickensian villain. In the subsequent years, with all the muckraking tabloid newspapers knocking on any door that might provide a story, they must've found him and he never uttered a word. This was at odds with my long-held image of my stepdad. It is unignorably principled and kind. This small recognition became the aperture through which a new dawn is beheld. The reality that I hold within, is not absolute, it is a construct. If it does not serve me, if it is not objectively authentic, then why not change it? The light of this new dawn thaws the cold intransigent past. Then a coincidence.

Anyone that has worked this program will tell you how often coincidences occur – how frequently people that you need to meet are put in front of you, how you encounter 'signs'. It can be kind of annoying as the spooky reverence people give to these events is part of the limp New Age airy-fairy aspect of spirituality that many find understandably repellent. Nevertheless, I have found that since I have begun to place less prominence on materialism and my own egotistical demands of the world, coincidences have occurred more frequently. Or at least have seemed to, who cares? In this case I was visiting Great Ormond Street Children's Hospital (didn't I mention it? I'm a pretty great guy) and standing at the foot of the first bed of the first ward of this vast institution I was taken to, was my stepdad's nephew. His son was the patient. We chatted and I asked him about my stepdad, he gave me his number. I was able to reach out by phone and he didn't respond to texts or calls, indicating that, understandably, he didn't want anything to do with me. I wrote him a letter taking full responsibility for my actions, offering to make amends in any way that he saw fit.

I apologized and wished him well and asked if I could do anything for him. I didn't hear back, but now view the relationship differently. I have amended my attitude to him and with it my perception of the past and my behaviour going forward. I now acknowledge that I am often wrong in my interpretations of other people's behaviour and that I am better off not to judge them at all: an approach that would have been inconceivable to the person I used to be, the person I am when not working a program, the person I default to. The amends step is an indication of change, real change. At points it does feel like I'm 'going through the motions' but this in itself facilitates authentic personal development, 'Fake it till you make it', they often say.

In my previous life and I suspect in the lives of many reading this book, little reference is made to spirit and conscious ritual. Mostly we are engaged in material pursuits of one kind or another, the many obligations of ordinary life having ensnared and enslaved. It's not easy to float about like a Sufi if you've got three kids and a mortgage or you're trying to get promoted to pay extortionate urban rent. Much of that upon which happiness depends is beyond mechanistic definition; the machinations of the mind and spirit cannot be easily measured. In Step 9, I felt the palpable presence of the sacred each time I made a 'face-to-face' amends. The structure of the language that the protocol suggests acts as a secular spell, summoning ethereal witness. As if a gently burning circle or an impromptu chapel appears on uttering these apparently quite unremarkable words:

> 'As you know, I am an addict. Part of the process of my recovery from addiction is that I must make amends to those I have wronged. I have wronged you and I owe you an amends.'

This simple sentence is the entry point to your face-to-face amends and somehow its words form an arch through which you walk into a quieter space, a space that is not just occupied by you and the other person. It is as if somehow something has been evoked, some hidden principle. Each time I have done it I have felt a subtle awe and unbidden tearfulness. I have felt humbled, I have felt the grace that occurs when you decide to put aside your own way of doing things and surrender to another way.

That said, it is a practical measure that can be deployed more bureaucratically. Some people suggest the rather more prosaic introduction: 'Periodically I review my life to determine if I have harmed anybody. I feel I may have harmed you' with no reference to spirituality or particular addictions. If you are conducting this process because you would like to engage with a more purposeful life without addressing any specific behaviour, this form is appropriate. This is the suggested structure:

1 Tell the person the harm, focused and to the point, no excuses.
2 Ask the person if they want to comment or if they'd like to add anything else, then shut up and listen (I find that part especially hard).
3 Suggest the amends you'd like to make.
4 Ask the person if the amends is acceptable or if they'd like additional or different amends.

The amends you offer ought to be commensurate with the harm done. With my MTV friend, who I'd denied access to my work cab account which I'd elsewhere misused with selfish abandon, I met up with him, apologized as described above and organized a flash car to pick him up from work and drive him home. This is what you might call a 'light-hearted' amends. Nonetheless when I think back to my shame regarding the selfishness of my earlier actions this personal ritual has assuaged my self-loathing and healed the damage between us. Don't worry about him, he writes for Ant 'n' Dec these days, he's having a gay ol' time.

> Have you had someone apologize to you, a fellow driver or a life partner who has said, "I'm sorry *you feel* I was rude to you?" When I get those apologies I want to shove the apologizer into a ravine. It's not a *mea culpa*, it's a *you-a-culpa*.'

My amends to my parents and a number of ex-girlfriends were rather less jocund. They consisted of a frank, quiet apology and a commitment to being a different man going forward. My relationships with my parents have radically improved and are clear and honest now. It is worth reflecting again at this point that this program has now been applied to dozens of addictions. It amazes me still that once beyond the initial acknowledgement of our inability to control the behaviour or substance in question, we tackle an issue that is far beyond it: the way we relate to ourselves and others and life more broadly. We embrace our life as something to be pursued with purpose, not blindly and unconsciously endured.

What is actually happening when I make amends to work colleagues or exes? Who or what am I actually communing with? In a sense it is myself, I am committing to being a different man, to myself. Have you ever inadvertently made amends to someone, tearfully or perhaps drunkenly? Or sheepishly apologized to a slighted friend, aware of the need but unsure of how to do it? I have – simple guidelines such as 'Don't make excuses for your behaviour' and 'Let them speak' would've made a world of difference. Have you had someone apologize to you, a fellow driver or a life partner who has said, 'I'm sorry *you feel* I was rude to you?' When I get those apologies I want to shove the apologizer into a ravine. That is because this program merely formalizes what we all spiritually intuit, that there is a way to make an apology, and that apologizing for 'making a person feel' something, instead of for what you did is not a *mea culpa*, it's a *you-a-culpa*.

Some Step 9s can't be made because 'to do so would injure them or others'. The point of doing these steps is to make us useful, I hesitate to say happy because happiness, to me, seems like such wet-gummed frivolity, dumb and fleeting. If you think about it too much it'll disappear, like an erection. Usefulness. Purpose. These ideas are robust enough to weather the turbulent meteorology of the mind. If making a particular amends will harm the person you are making it to, don't make it. If it would give them information that would be painful to them or if seeing you again would be traumatic, refrain. These potential complications are further demonstration of the necessity for guidance in this process. I talk through each instance on Step 8 with my mentor and what I propose as an amends. This means that me and my crazy ol' 'caused-all-these-problems-in-the-first place' brain are not being entrusted with the means of resolution. Similarly, if making an amends might land you in jail it should be approached with extreme caution. We should be willing to deal with the consequences of our actions, and many practitioners of this program say that willingness to go to 'any lengths' to change means we should be prepared to face even jail. In my personal experience there was little of a criminal nature that needed to be amended, stealing from MTV is a crime, obviously I was using illicit drugs, but most of my 'Wrongs' amounted to cheating and exploiting people and being incredibly selfish. Under guidance I still concluded that a good many people would best be addressed by letter, that the last thing they'd want was me, looming back into their lives with combed hair and good intentions.

I didn't believe my promiscuity was wrong for the many years that it governed my life. I thought it was acceptable. I knew I had little control over it and at my core sensed it had more to do with lacking love, connection and meaning than chasing orgasms, but I certainly didn't think I was harming anyone else. Now I know that by participating in another person's unconscious behaviour, especially if it is destructive or harming to their self-esteem, I am participating in their pain. This is all the more troubling because, when awakened, I have an opportunity to assist their healing.

Some people didn't want any further contact with me, which I have to accept as a consequence of my behaviour. Some people, and this is common, were embarrassed by the process but still grateful. My first ever Step 9 was with Matt Morgan, a dear friend who I used with and worked with a lot, arguably causing him a lot more harm in the second phase of my addiction than in the earlier and more obvious substance-misuse phase. I made amends to him in my room at a posh London hotel. Matt took the bizarre measure of holding a cushion in front of his face as I tried to remain pious. In this case the 'Wrongs' I was seeking to atone for were: giving him drugs, involving him in a seedy and unpleasant world of addiction and being controlling and obstructive around our work together. Matt, when he emerged from behind the cushion, said he had no problem with the sex and drugs stuff but that he did feel aggrieved by my controlling work behaviour, even listing examples of harm done to him that I myself had forgotten. The fact that it is challenging for the recipient as well as the person making the amends is, I believe, a testament to its authenticity. People know that something real is happening. We live in a world that is dominated by rationalism, where emotions are often excluded. In Victorian Britain, as industrialization and urbanization consumed the land, several of London's rivers were submerged beneath paving and concrete so the teeming flow couldn't interrupt the mechanical march. Beneath the concrete of our conditioning flow the rivers of our better nature, awaiting liberation.

The majority of my amends were scheduled but there were occasions where a 'surprise', 'on the spot' Step 9 was required. In my professional life a good many people were hurt when I severed relationships believing they were no longer useful to me. This was often done in an irresponsible way that caused harm. One man who had promoted my live work for a long time had been coldly dispatched without explanation and was very hurt. I had never acknowledged the harm I had done him and didn't really think about it. A mutual friend told me that I had caused suffering and once aware, it played on my mind and I began to see how I had transgressed, that I had been selfish and irresponsible. One night at a live show I ran into him. An indication that, on some level, I knew I had done wrong was that I felt a churning in my guts on seeing him. It was my own neglected code that I was not abiding by, not a learned dogma. My body viscerally let me know that I needed to make amends, not a blank and learned moral code.

This step is about making ourselves right with the world. So many of us are encumbered with fear and shame, these feelings are affirmed if we can't go out into the world without running into wounded people who understandably regard us unfavourably. It becomes easy to see that our relationships with people become the instantiations of negative attitudes to ourselves: I believe myself to be ugly; I behave in an ugly way; I then have relationships with others that confirm my belief. A self-perpetuating doctrine. The person I used to be, on sighting a person with whom there was bad blood, would either avoid the person or 'front' the situation out. Like most people, I did not want to change; I wanted to justify staying the same. 'If you had my childhood, my problems, my mental illness then you would behave like this too.' This though, is a program of change. You accept you want to change, you believe change is possible, you become willing to receive input from new sources – possibly the group, possibly a mentor, possibly a Higher Power, ideally all three – and then you examine where you've been going wrong, share it and commit to new attitudes. This completed you start to deal with all the damage you've done while living by your previous program, usually a clumsily accreted bundle of clichés and responses to abuse and trauma.

I felt sick when I ran into my former colleague but I knew what I had to do. I humbly approached him and said I had something I needed to tell him if he had the time. Given it was a comedy gig at the Apollo Theatre in London and he was promoting it he would've been well within his rights to avoid this uncomfortable conversation. Instead he said 'Sure', and when he had a moment he led me to a backstage office. In the interim I had found time to pray in a toilet. This may seem peculiar to a modern secular person but most of us recognize this impulse, the occasional need to 'have a word' with ourselves. I know I did, long before I regarded it as spiritual. My whole life I've been locking myself in toilets to summon up a transcendent experience of one kind or another: as a kid gorging on chocolate and then puking it up, then frenetically spellbound by porn, then drugs, then finally prayer. In every instance the need was the same, to get out of my head, to feel a connection, to feel something beyond being me in a body, on a planet, in infinite space. I contest that we all have this yearning for connection, even if from a humanist perspective. What is the numinous jolt we feel when witnessing the heroic sacrifice of another? Or the tearful pull when people come together in a common cause? What string is being plucked when we encounter heroism? Could it be that we are reminded by the hero's sacrifice that the appearance of individualism is temporal? That when the hero sees beyond this artificial world of selfish wants and needs, and falls in faith, into the arms of the Ulterior Oneness, we are reminded and relieved? What is the value of fraternity? What is solidarity's power? What manner of virtue is kindness if it is not the acknowledgement that in truth and in fact we are all one, together here, and what we do to each other we do to ourselves? Heroism's power is in redolence. It reminds us what we've always known but forgotten: we are all connected.

In prayer at the Apollo I appeal to this Oneness. I steel myself with the knowledge that when walking this path I am no longer a cluster of cells and wants, a priapic and salivating happiness maximizer, I am attempting to tune into the mainframe. He leads me into the office. It is loud outside because the act is about to go on stage but in the room it is quiet. I speak with as low a voice as circumstances allow, taking responsibility for my actions precisely as the step suggests. Then it is his turn to talk. He tells me of the pain caused by my cold severance, of the consequences it had for him and his career and his private life. Listening to this I feel vulnerable, I viscerally feel how my unconscious and uncaring behaviour has caused this man to suffer. It is good for me to listen to this. It is good for me to acknowledge that it hurts me to have hurt him, that I cannot close the door on the suffering of others. I silently stand and take it. When he has finished I ask if there is anything I can do for him, he's a pretty masculine northern bloke and predictably says he's 'Fine ta very much'. Afterwards I feel a little perturbed as I join my friends at the gig, uncertain in my anxiety as to whether it was the right thing to do, raking up the past, reopening old wounds. Does it do me any good? Did it do him any good? Before the comic comes on stage though, my former colleague reappears and noticeably awkward, but with kindly deliberation, presents me with four after-show passes. In the muted language of men of a certain background and age this constitutes forgiveness. He moves on quite brusquely but perhaps a little healed. Certainly he had no need to seek me out with an additional gesture of goodwill. I know that how I treated him and the many other people on my list was wrong. I know too that I am not a bad person, I was a person who had lost my way but with the program I no longer need to harm myself or others.

The last ten years of my life have been carried out publicly, romances, a marriage, scandals and controversy. I have sought to work this step wherever I could. Sometimes amends are general. A broad personal observation is that since being relieved of my epic, grandiose and all-consuming substance misuse the drives that fuelled it have easily

> My working an amends process is not a mechanical means to get myself back onto Father Christmas's "Nice List", it is an attempt to align myself with an inner attention that exists unbidden within me and informs me when it is not being "heard" by making me feel bad.'

been channelled into my sexual, romantic and professional life. In these areas then I have not been living according to my Higher Self. That doesn't mean my behaviour has been uniformly bad, I have had one-night stands that were characterized by tremendous honesty and tenderness. I have had professional relationships and experiences that have bordered on the sublime. In both of these areas though, there were streams of my life where adrenaline and excess are seen as permissible. If, as I was, you are a young and famous man, having sex with lots of women is encouraged. If you are temperamental in your working life, given to erratic outbursts and emotional crashes, this will be tolerated for as long as you are making people money. Remember we are not discussing the breach of external codes or laws here, we are not talking about illegal activity, corruption, theft or non-consensual relationships – those carry their own social penalties. We are talking about our own inner code, innate and ignored while we transgress but perennially present. I can see now that if I am physically using a woman, when I know that it will be of no benefit to either of us, beyond short-term pleasure – which is, let's face it, an extremely effective and diverting reward system – then I am participating in 'bad faith' activity. This is because I now know that I cannot be fulfilled by transient pleasures and that as an awakening man, my attitude towards women is to be one of nurture, kindness and generosity. My condition led me to see everyone and everything as a resource. This was not calculated, it was unconscious. I didn't, in the swirl of eye contact with a beautiful woman, inwardly cackle like a vampire, I was simply lulled into dumb fulfilment by the current of a continual unconscious drive. From a Step 9 perspective this pattern was conducted for too long a period for direct amends to be appropriate, also, for a recovering sex addict in a monogamous relationship, it is inadvisable to go skipping down memory lane equipped with doe-eyed apologies and good intentions, into the company of previous lovers. My amends in this area are 'living amends', which means I no longer view women in the way I once did, neither do I conduct myself in that manner. Furthermore I actively look for opportunities to be of assistance to women in appropriate ways. In my case this means selflessly and, where possible, with complete anonymity. Believe me, I'd like nothing more than at this point to divulge a litany of worthy women's causes of which I am a proud benefactor, but I'm too spiritual, so you'll just have to take my word for it.

Amie, as a former sex worker, chronic addict and beloved friend, provides me with the perfect opportunity to make a general amends to women. Not for women, although my changing attitude and behaviour will I'm sure be beneficial to others, it is for myself that this process is taken. To move me into alignment with a higher vision of myself. The tension, guilt and sadness I feel when living in addiction is to me an indication of an awareness that there is another way of being. A higher, preferable way. I don't believe these are taught social codes, or petit bourgeois ideals. I believe this to be a marrow-deep, helix-hard presence that wants to realize itself in the same way that a tree is moving to self-realization from the moment the seed splits. Perhaps before, perhaps it is an unbroken spiral of root and branch reaching through what we call 'time' back to the creation of life itself.

So my working an amends process is not a mechanical means to get myself back onto Father Christmas's 'Nice List', it is an attempt to align myself with an inner attention that exists unbidden within me

> Now obviously there are people who can devastate their lives through sex and gambling and others who can use crack relatively consequence-free, but as a general guide, the more you learn about addiction, and the craving and thinking that accompany it, the more these divisions seem redundant, the distinctions melt away.'

and informs me when it is not being 'heard' by making me feel bad. This is different I think from transgressing a taught social code, like using the wrong knife with the wrong hand at the wrong banquet. Perhaps the flush of shame we feel when we breach external protocols references this resource, but how we treat each other – how we manifest or deny love – I feel relates to a deeper force even than our primal drives and appetites.

If this were a pop science book, I'd now regale you with tales of the oxytocin ballet and dopamine dance that takes place when we are altruistic or in proximity to our beloved, but this biochemical analysis amounts to a fashionable and semantically novel reworking of what yogis, sages, Sufis and saints have been telling us for millennia as the result of their limitless work in laboratories that are subtler than those forged in concrete and glass: love is the answer.

Amie in the house comes with a poltergeist. She brings the spirit of addiction with her, like a floating contagion. Even the way that the Weetabix box looks, cast to the side like someone has interfered with it at a bus stop. She is the ultra-addict, it's curled up in her like a cat without fur, purring quietly. She's a frightened and frightening child. I am agitated when she's here and when she's gone, knowing that she is patient zero, knowing she carries it in its purest form. I'm cautious the day after she leaves, the spare room almost cordoned off with yellow tape. I feel like I breathe the tail of the ghost. I feel it in me when she's passed. I find myself bathed in fridge light eating chocolate I don't remember wanting and my thoughts turn to porn, insidious thoughts not like the lumpen and clumsy addiction of my youth, ham-fisted wanks and heroin. Now this fiend armed with my intellect could trick me into the sewers unnoticed.

Preceding even my first thought, there it sits in my gut and my bones, the lazy contagion. My dreams are a grey playground but I never want to leave them, even for the heavenly wonder of my family home. The addiction sits there quietly in my gut, like a timeless affiliate of all the addiction that has gone before. Impersonal. Beyond me and beneath me. It feels so physical, that's why I suppose the call to action is so strong, either to get high or drunk or to have sex, something that changes the way that I feel.

Amie got eighteen months clean from heroin at a BAC treatment facility in the Midlands, in the UK. She is not every pale face on an escalator, every glum staring gridlock prisoner nursing an addiction to spending, work, porn or relationships. She is, in fact, a pamphlet addict. Jarringly beautiful, her battle with addiction takes place in an identifiable and obvious context, lit up by her face.

In the ten years that I've known her Amie has had a year, six months, maybe even two years clean at different times. One of her most devastating relapses took place while she was a first-year student at drama school. Her attainment of a place at one of the most prestigious drama schools in the world, where a handful of students per year are selected from thousands of applicants, is a staggering achievement. This is a woman who has known suffering usually confined to people from other countries and other centuries. Epic abuse and dispossession. For her heroin addiction was a sensible response to unendurable pain.

'Consumerism and materialism are creating a culture of addiction. We are all on the scale somewhere because we are kept there by the age we live in.'

During the third term of her course, she relapsed hard, blood on cubicle walls, gouching out in classrooms, grant money all spent on drugs, and she had to leave. This was painful as a spectator, let alone as a protagonist, confirmation of the thumping supremacy of this disease against all ornamentation and seeming success. Over the next three years Amie got clean again, mostly in the same BAC facility where she lived and worked. Group therapy, individual therapy, community integration, personal responsibility, all that. She reapplied to drama school, did the necessary four auditions to get to the final round, made her peace with the shocked and disappointed staff. Then the Friday before the Monday's 'shoo-in' audition relapsed on crack and heroin.

Amie went quiet in the days before her final audition: cagey, AWOL, politely dismissive texts. When the calamitous news came from a third party, as a euphemistic enquiry, 'Have you spoken to Amie?' I barely had the energy to sigh. I met her the next day on Finchley Road, a thankless dual carriageway, and along she came, made of broken branches, a dim film over her. Departed. I asked her to talk me through the events and how the events related to thoughts and where the fork in the road occurred, where the departure took place and the answer surprised me.

Amie had naturally been excited about her drama school audition and the prospect of reclaiming a lost opportunity. Drama school became in the parlance of recovery her 'Higher Power', the thing that was going to make life alright. For an addict this is a big no-no. You cannot ever elect an ersatz totem, a false idol. Of course we want to,

I do it every ten seconds. It could be a part in a film, a passing stranger or a can of Diet Coke – 'If I get that, I'll be alright', I think, not those words, it's quicker and more insidious than words. It's just a shift of attention and intention from the understanding that I am here to be useful to the idea that I am an objective-pursuing robot.

Understandably the lonely and damaged little girl that Amie to some degree will always be thought that if she could get into drama school (again!) everything would be okay. This became her focus. She said she felt both excited and afraid and that she couldn't control her feelings so she started to manage her moods through her eating, bingeing and vomiting. In addict world, if you are a declared addict you'll know this, there is a clear, if totally unfair, hierarchy of addictions. The worst (therefore best) addiction is intravenous heroin addiction. Then crack and heroin, smoked together. Then a tier where booze, pills and weed all rattle around. Then food, gambling and sex. Then relationships and work.

Now obviously there are people who can devastate their lives through sex and gambling and others who can use crack relatively consequence-free, but as a general guide, superficially, that is the Champions League, mid-table, relegation struggler shape of the situation. The more you learn about addiction, and the craving and thinking that accompany it, the more these divisions seem redundant, the distinctions melt away. That is why we shouldn't be surprised that Amie, a lifelong hard drug user from the top tier, unthinkingly became obsessed with 'work', then food before, on the Friday, 'I was puking up into the toilet having eaten a load of chocolate when the thought occurred to me that if I'm doing this, all this puking, crouching over a toilet, I might as well be using. I went down to the cashpoint, drew out two hundred quid, went to this estate in Hackney where I see this homeless couple and said I'd get them a couple of bags if they'd get me five of each.'

Amie had eighteen months clean when she made that decision. In that moment the idea of calling another addict for help, or willpower, or the promise of a bright future treading the boards were all swept away by the private tide of addiction. What does that craving want? What manner of impulse is this that has evolved? An instinct to destroy the host vessel. Total self-destruction.

Amie is interesting because in the inflated, bloated grotesqueness of her condition we might be able to see patterns that are invisible in less obvious cases, I would maintain though that the shape, the template, is uniform. How does this example relate to Carl Jung's verdict that what chronic addicts need is a spiritual experience and ongoing communal support? How does it relate to the 12 Step movements that began in the United States, inspired by Jung's insight, in the decades that followed?

Anyone who suffers from food issues knows how total and dreadful it is. Family members feel the same stranded impotence that a drug addict's family feels. Gamblers that have crossed over know the helplessness, shame and despair that this condition brings. These are the outliers, in whom the universal condition is acute and therefore observable. Our natural yearnings are running amok and they are being stirred and nourished by a society that uses our desire as its fuel. Consumerism and materialism are creating a culture of addiction. We are all on the scale somewhere because we are kept there by the age we live in.

Junkies like Amie are at the inverted summit. Her name twists the knife. Amy Winehouse was similar to Amie, similar in that she was somehow housed in the heavens and the gutter. In that she could make your jaw drop with her gift and your heart sink with her affliction. When Amy died and I blamed myself, perhaps vainly, for not having 'done something', I said to myself, I swore in fact, that

Amie would not go the same way. As if I have that kind of power. She ricochets between worlds. One name is not enough for this addict, I never meet the woman that goes out and uses. I am never able to intercept her. I only meet the agonizingly demure and sweetly repentant woman who wants to recover. When the darkness comes, she retreats like an animal. In Amie I watch from the sidelines as the efficacy of the program is played out: will she, won't she? She may yet die from this condition. I sometimes despair. I sometimes think 'Maybe it's inevitable'. In her I see that this way is not some life improvement method, like hair gel for a soul that needs styling. It is doing the job that religion is once said to have done. People – me, and probably you – also need total change, we need epiphany, we need transcendence but we really dig TV, so we defer. I can get away with a day of selfish thinking and dumb distraction, I mean I feel like shit but it doesn't kill me. Amie though is going to have to get to redemption through a narrow gap. This program can create that space.

In some people 'the call' is strong, they need either hard drugs or hard recovery. Hard recovery means 'No more bullshit'. No more little kicks and fixes, nothing that can take you away from the connection: the truth; the purpose; the oneness; the moment. It means that this, Recovery, is now the framework for the experience of being you. Not pleasure, or envy, or passing memes and pipedreams, no it is this system, a system that is designed to change your perspective, give you a connection and then a purpose to maintain it. In Step 9 we make restitution that in our old life, our old plan, we would never have countenanced. It is a fine example of the broader 12 Step philosophical trope that 'You can't think your way into acting better but you can act your way into thinking better'. Under the guidance of a mentor, with the support and community of other people on the same path, you have, by following the actions suggested by this program, broken loose from your prior confinement and become a different person. Whilst Step 9 seems to be about making amends to others it is we who are amended.

Step 9 Exercises: Now apologize. Unless that would make things worse.

We don't make amends if in doing so we'd cause additional harm. An obvious example: if you've had an affair with a person who is in a relationship, you don't saunter into their parlour and sob all over their doilies, telling them you've been diddling their husband. No one is helped by that.

But you can't use this clause as a way to avoid amends that you ought to make, like a crafty and brilliant barrister. In 12 Step legend there are burglars that have risked imprisonment by going back to the houses they have robbed and making amends to the occupant. You should follow the guidance of a mentor, the person that helped you through the steps to this point and start with the many amends that are free from complexity.

The instructions are simple. Discuss each potential amends with a mentor.

Then:

Meet with the person, tell them the harm, apologize, offer an appropriate amends (if it's financial it's obvious, generally the amends is to evoke the opposite feeling of the harm), ask if they have anything to add and if they think your amends is satisfactory.

Your general demeanour ought to be calm and humble.

The experience varies depending on the nature of the harm and the recipient of the amends. When I have done it I have often felt a deeper connection with my negative behaviour and the consequences of my actions for others. In conducting the amends I have seen how I am changing, amending, becoming a different man.

Ask yourself:

- Am I willing to change?
- Am I willing to be changed in ways I may not be aware of or in control of?
- Am I willing to address each harm that I am aware of?
- Am I being completely honest with my mentor about the nature of the harm?
- Have I thoroughly prepared each amend with a mentor?
- Am I willing to complete all my amends using creative solutions for individuals I can't meet?
- Is finishing my amends a top priority in my life?
- Have I finished my amends? Am I avoiding some?

10

Watch out for fucked up thinking and behaviour and be honest when it happens.

Step 10: We continued to take personal inventory and when we were wrong promptly admitted it.

Step 10 is the first of what are colloquially known as 'the maintenance steps', that means we work them on a daily basis. Taking personal inventory is something I've always had a good deal of resistance to, perhaps because the person who needs to comply with the instruction to take inventory is precisely the kind of indolent and obstinate tool who will not do it. The principle that serves with this step is 'awareness'. I am learning to watch myself, I am learning to spot the moment when I give up my inner connection, my serenity, and leap into my 'beast' nature. Or when I move from conscious connection to unconscious disconnection. I can be strolling along a twee high street, butterflies aflutter about me, auric streams of lavender wonder encircling me, when I'll see a fellow human being's arse. This sends an immediate and disruptive signal to my orbitofrontal cortex; the butterflies drop like sleet, the aura turns purple and I have a decision to make. The decision is not whether or not to do anything, like wolf-whistle – I'm not a sociopath in a seventies sitcom – the decision is what to do with my thoughts. Do I leap into the synaptic tornado of potential fantasy or do I work Step 10? Have I conceded to my innermost self that my life now is no longer a vessel into which I pack pleasure and satisfaction? Have I relinquished the idea that I can ever be fulfilled by fleeting, physical phenomena?

'You think about things very deeply Russell,' said my Auntie Janet to me one Christmas. I was fraught about something, likely perturbed by the unfamiliarity of the crammed familial setting, always happier tethered to my mother's apron strings. Here in father's world I floundered for means. I don't remember what I said to prompt my Auntie Janet's analysis but I know that people have always thought that I think too much or too quickly or too deeply and I can see why. I can see that in our normal world of TMZ and online shopping and glib immediacy, the sighting of a pleasant bottom and its impulsive accompaniment of desire would not be the starting pistol for an expedition of self-discovery. But for we who are discontented here, this is the road we must travel. No point bemoaning what everyone else 'gets away with'. In this world people seem to be getting away with a lot; a lot of consuming, a lot of gratification, a lot of senseless sensuality, a lot of bilious materialism, wilful indifference to suffering, selfishness and dishonesty but for you and me this is not the way. It can never work for us. We will never wrestle bliss from this world. We settle for pleasure and we never discover bliss. 'This world has nothing else to give you now Russell, it can only take away from you,' said the bearded swami, all glowing and swathed in ochre. My gut squirmed before my face reframed on hearing these words. 'I know this.' It is more a recollection rather than new teaching; 'Yes, that's it, there it is,' some inner voice says to the returning truth as it rejoins us, like a bird alighting on the bare branch within. A new shaft of light, another corner of darkness illuminated. Nothing new, just the rediscovery of a neglected part of you.

Now when I am attracted to a woman and my old code jolts with the sudden snap of a stirring crocodile, my new program is fired up. Not with the slick efficiency of an immaculate Apple app. No, like a whirring and whistling Victorian time machine, juddering into clumsy life, blinking and twitching and setting off bells. To do this I must have an inner connection of some kind, an awareness. If I am falling forward through life, some inert berk zombie-ing along, I'll cling to any branch I come across. If I am aware, I have a throne within me, I have a personal sovereignty from where I can adjudicate. 'I could stare at this person,' I think as the scaly and serpentine missile shatters the wall of my sanctum, 'But then what? Then I will be flooded with desire. The desire will want me to breach my own ideals, which, if I do, will have consequences, inner and outer, and if I don't do, will disturb my peace. I know this is an illusion. That I can

> I am learning to watch myself, I am learning to spot the moment when I give up my inner connection, my serenity, and leap into my "beast" nature. I have awakened to the truth of what my life is and is not. It is a chance to be connected to limitless and eternal beauty, it is not a theme park for my dick.'

never be contented by carnal pleasure, that I have awakened to the truth of what my life is and is not. It is a chance to be connected to limitless and eternal beauty, it is not a theme park for my dick.'

Here I petition my Self, my Higher Consciousness, this newly awakened experiencer of thoughts and feelings to provide me with power. I am referring to the self as divided, a Higher Self and a lower self. Conventionally this lower self could be defined as 'ego', the mental object we consider ourselves to be before we undertake any serious analysis. In moments when we are unchallenged it is helpful to have clearly iterated ideals to which we are willing to work. That way we have immediate access to a checklist, as I keep saying much of the spiritual life as I live it is admin. In my case, I have written in each area of my life, a 'sound ideal' that I am committed to attaining. I am in a monogamous relationship. That means one of the 'roles' I have in life is as a 'boyfriend'. What is my *ideal* as a *boyfriend*, what am I working towards? This can be explicit, in my previous life everything was so vaguely understood that any manifesto could be rewritten, moment to moment, according to whimsy. Not these days baby! No, in my role as a boyfriend here is my explicit 'sound ideal':

I am loyal – that means no cheating (so what's the point of staring?).

I am kind – that means when my girlfriend is telling me something and I think, 'I'm not interested in this bullshit, when can we talk about me?' a second voice, that isn't crazy, is present to say, 'Psst, Russell, remember that ideal about being kind? This is precisely where it is applicable.'

I am generous – this means with my time and money and affection.

I am honest – honest, not stupid. I don't tell my girlfriend every fleeting thought I have, no one should be subjected to that. I suppose she might read this book, which is going to give her an insight she could probably do without. Though to be honest she is startlingly capable of ignoring my 'creative outpourings' (yuck) so we might be okay.

There are many more ideals, the key is to identify the areas where you yourself may struggle and then create an ideal that helps to counter that. If you are a hopeless codependent, forever fussing over your partner like a right little cling-on, you needn't emphasize 'attentive', you've got that for free. You may need to have an ideal that facilitates 'independence' or 'self-sufficiency'. This is why this program works, there is no doctrine, there is no guru; you are your own teacher based on what you learn through a process of admission, honesty and confession. You will undertake this process with guidance but not under tutelage. You will have the support of a community but you will not suppress your individuality. This process brings you into line with the unexpressed and strangulated yearning to be whole that, if you're like me, you've been woefully misinterpreting your whole life.

Also there are numerous roles. In my life I have been assigned roles as: a father, a boyfriend, a work colleague, a road user, a gym member, a son, a friend. In each of these roles I now have designated ideals and if ever conflict arises, or I feel discontent, I can mentally or literally check the list. This is a more conscious way of living. It is also highly practical. It's not just a wing and a prayer. It is often said that you read a manual for a new TV (I don't) but live life without instruction. As our trusted external institutions and social contracts all melt away, it is more important than ever to live by a personal code.

I find this hard. Inventorying, then, is a daily, possibly constant process of instantiation of new ideals. From this emergent place of awareness we observe our fluctuations and leanings. Even in pleasant mundanity I become untethered from peace and my mind becomes a quick and prickling safari of incessant tricky assessment and judgement. A life of bucolic wonder can become *Apocalypse Now* inside my mind. Even in my idyllic life with my dog Bear. Bear is enthusiasm with claws. We have a rowboat and I heap Bear in. The river is so alive with light and dark. On the surface light dances like spilt heaven and if you put your feet in, the sludge and slime feels like the ooze that we crawled out of. The whole spectrum is there, the river is the whole road, the beginning, the end, ever changing, ever present. Is the river the water or its cradle?

And on we row, Bear and I, having loudly discussed the seating arrangements till I dump him over my shoulder like a sack of himself because I couldn't organize my legs for purchase. Whenever another boat passes though I feel a bit too aware and its wake spreads towards the bank disruptively. We clatter into some branches from beneath and the Bear meets this horror with the same tongue-lolling wonder that he greets all stimuli. We crunch our way back out and wind the many bends to the Lilliputian shore where Bear and I often play. Here though in addition to the sprawled and infinite goose shit, that Bear if undistracted will vacantly chomp, is a Perfect Beach Tribe. Three men, like models look when they've deliberately cast models who don't look too modelly – one with a big beard and another with slightly crooked teeth. In this case it is Bill, who has both the beard and the teeth, and a quiet and focused Chinese wife, naked daughter

179

and baby son. Then there is Harry, straight from a Greek urn via an Australian soap, hair drips from his head in golden curls, like a honey volcano went off in his brain and Tom. Tom is big and though I don't know it yet will shake my hand in that way that makes me feel I've something to prove.

I am afraid.

The Perfect Beach Tribe are busy but cool. They're not showing off. I nearly just keep rowing. Mooring here will mean interaction. The fear is not pronounced. People call it 'angst' but I need clarity. Fear. I don't immediately read it, it's down in the weeds, it's not told my brain it's there yet but my legs know. The Perfect Beach Tribe have two dogs. One kind of Chihuahua and one kind of part-Staff thing. They bark a lot. I decide I will moor because if I don't moor it would mean I was afraid and I don't want to be afraid, so I moor to prove it.

I drag our little fibreglass vessel the last few inches and Bear rolls out and throws up his dopey hackles like some webbed novelty in *Jurassic Park*. I speak calmly as Tom, who is big, rearranges his dogs, eventually dumping them into their perfect tribal boat. This is all done with minimum fuss. The fear is quiet. The fear is a quiet and overzealous signal, 'Be alert'. The fear, the awareness of the wound, the implicit memory; the recollections of times where similar visual signifiers have preceded humiliation, shame and embarrassment – at school the bigger boys, the cooler crowd, themselves an echo of otherness's potential malevolence. The reality of the Perfect Beach Tribe (PBT) is not something I can experience objectively. All I know is how they look to me. All I know is how I feel, and that is all I'll ever know unless I can learn a new system for being.

Bill comes over and says hello while I stand now on the goose shit beach vaguely embarrassed by Bear's looping enthusiasm. 'I heard you on Joe Rogan,' he says. Joe Rogan, a former mixed martial arts fighter, commentator and host of the world's most downloaded podcast is himself an interesting example of new emerging models of masculinity. A fusion of seemingly right-wing individualism and new age tolerance, a fierce autodidact, he has become a champion of American libertarianism and is to me fascinating because he is clever and a fighter.

When someone politely tells me they've experienced something I've done in the public eye, it's a social relaxant. Without drinking or drugs I hum with spikey awareness. We chat for a while and Bill says he studied at the School of Oriental and African Studies, SOAS, where I mentioned I was going to do a Master's degree in Joe's podcast. We talk for a while about Joseph Campbell and religion while the other members of the perfect tribe pack up their camp. To me these people seem at ease. Bill and his wife and two children, Tom and his two dogs, Harry and his perfect stomach and stand up paddle board, which is like a modern Huck Finn raft and which they insist I have a go on and which, in a demonstration of great change, I actually do. I stand on this inflatable plank with a paddle that's much too short and precariously drift across the idyllic Thames. I am standing on water and I do some mandatory Jesus jokes and point to my own tee-shirt on which the Son of God is shown doing just that in fact, walking on water.

I can be very anxious about people. Sometimes I look at the appointments I have, social and otherwise, and wish I could cancel the lot. Sometimes I do, and then on my prized couch, TV on, the place I was aiming for, I sit with the same anxiety lightly bubbling. Why is this? What does the feeling want?

I have to discard the prejudice I'd instantly conjured for each individual in turn as I meet them. Harry, too good-looking, can't share his paddle board quickly enough. Tom too tough-looking and shook my hand too hard – just a side note here, I'm not one of those who does the ghostly wet, shuddery molestation of a handshake, I love firm, but a handshake needn't surely be an act of bone-crunching war. Tom did not take it to that place but it was one notch down and frankly, because of his proportions, I was ready and waiting to adjudge him a bullyboy, but he is sweet and makes several kind attempts at connection.

The wife seems to be sealed in a capsule of motherhood and whether that's the reality or my perception is impossible to tell. Either way I am not triggered by her busy indifference in the same way I am by the tiny interactions with the males of the tribe. The interaction with these strangers, this vignette, this tableau, this reality that I experience briefly and through the clouded lens of my neurosis, contains many messages for me. When they finish packing up their cool camping kit into their long elegant boat – strewn with cushions, perfectly fitted with soft royal blue velvet seats, honestly, no roof, perfect, painted beautifully, rich mahogany wood, a silver wheel at the side, not the centre, to steer – the dogs, the babies, the woman, the men, the trailing aquatic toys purr off into forever in silence as the engine is electric. I sit on the bank and watch them go in private awe. Perfect normalness. Everyone so certain of their role, the mother, the dogs, the babies, the men.

I don't know what their 'reality' is. My psyche is talking to me through them, the image of them, the thought form of them as it hits the screen of my mind. My consciousness in conjunction with 'the outside world' is communicating something. My job is to understand the myth, to see where I am in the story of my life. All of us are having a unique experience here. Krishnamurti is right: 'Truth is a pathless land'; *Life Of Brian* is right: 'We are all individuals'. Materialism is right, consumerism is right, there is something that is uniquely you, inside of you. What we have to understand is who that is and what it wants. On the surface, nothing is happening but the inward coordinates manufacture a world in keeping with past patterns, fraught and fearful.

I heard it once said that the external world is like a movie that we watch; how often do you find yourself lost in that movie? How often is the connection between you and this new peace compromised? It could be a simple external stimulant, like a moment of road rage or a passing flirtation or it could even be your own thoughts. I can be alone in a room with nothing troubling in the diary or on the horizon and I'll suddenly start thinking about things that could go wrong in the future: 'What if there's a war?' 'What if my girlfriend leaves me?' I then react to these self-generated monsters. Sometimes instead, if all is relatively serene in the present, I'll slip off into the past and dredge up some painful memories and give them an airing out, see if I can't beat myself up that way. Step 9, which deals with the 'wreckage of the past', will alleviate this, but I have found that I can still pick up a cudgel from the annals and give myself a good battering. (Cudgel? Annal? Battering? And that's still not a euphemism.)

Structurally, a written Step 10 is identical to Step 4. There are four columns. In the first you write the person, place or thing that is causing you to be agitated. In the second column you put the resentment itself, in the third how it affects you and in the fourth, your part.

In this moment I have a resentment against my girlfriend. She has friends downstairs while I am trying to write. Let's see how Step 10 tackles this.

This affects my:

Pride
Not really.

Self-esteem
A little bit: why don't I like socializing? Why am I not the sort
of person who finds it easy? Why can't I drink? They are drinking
down there.

Personal relations
Maybe. Do I think Laura shouldn't have friends over because I am
working? Maybe a little bit.

Sexual relations
Maybe a little bit; maybe I think Laura puts energy into friendships
that she doesn't put into our sexual life.

Ambitions
I don't think so. Unless it's my ambition to have total control over
everyone at all times, which I'm beginning to see is unreasonable.

Security
Well I suppose I do need a lot of attention and customarily I like to
tacitly nominate my life partner to be the provider of that attention.

Finances
Yes, I'm worried about money, I've made a lot of professional changes
and, at the back of my mind, I'm worried that I won't be able to
fulfil my financial obligation as a provider, especially if there isn't an
atmosphere of hushed reverence around my working environment.

So I put all those into the third column:

I Resent	Because	This Affects My	My Part
Laura	She has friends round while I'm trying to write	SE, PR, SR, S, F	

Now let's see what my part is in the fourth column:

Where did I make a mistake?
Believing that I can or should control another person.

Where have I been selfish?
It is a bit selfish, she's just having some mates over.

Where was I dishonest?
Dishonest by omission; I think I myself should have a group of friends that come over as a unit.

Where was I self-seeking?
If it was up to me, everything all day would be about me, this is a resentment accrued due to that type of thinking.

Where was I afraid?
I am afraid that I will end up penniless and alone and if people knew the 'real me' they wouldn't like me.

Where am I to blame?
Not relevant in this instance.

Where am I at fault?
Not relevant here.

Where was I wrong?
Already covered.

And these all go into the fourth column:

I Resent	Because	This Affects My	My Part	
Laura	She has friends round while I'm trying to write	SE, PR, SR, S, F	1 Mistakes: Y 2 Selfishness: Y 3 Dishonesty: Y 4 Self-seeking: Y 5 Fears: Y 6 Blame: N 7 Fault: N 8 Wrong: N	

When spontaneously using this as an example I didn't realize that the thinking behind it would run so deep! I wasn't eaten up with resentment, stomping across my office floor (upstairs) sighing and making a scene. Thinking about it now, when her friends arrived, I did start shouting at the dog who was barking outside, which I now recognize as a displacement activity and an unconscious attempt to assert dominance. But as I say, I wasn't consciously that bothered. Nonetheless, my feelings of agitation were being motored by long-held, deep-seated fears and beliefs. I contest that in this I am no madder than you, that at points in any given day, you, like me, lose contact with your inner ideal, your Higher Self, and fall into an unacknowledged, pre-established pattern of 'being' that is detrimental to you and the people around you. Imagine a whole society run on these unaware drives, or save yourself the imaginary kilojoules and simply look at the one you live in, because that is what society does run on.

If I hadn't addressed that example I wouldn't have seen the seeds of my thinking. Luckily I haven't taken any radical action out in the world or I'd have to 'promptly admit' to the person or people that I'd upset that I was wrong. The next part of the step is to share it with someone I trust, not a romantic partner, a person with whom I have a spiritual agreement, a mentor. In admitting it to them I am also admitting it to myself and my Higher Power. I can then pray to have the defects, in this case selfishness and self-centredness, removed. Again, prayer could be regarded as a deep commitment to a Higher Self, a self that is no longer willing to lurk in the unexamined mire of unconscious drives and fear: an ideal self.

Over the course of a day I will be disturbed many times. I can mentally conduct this exercise if it is a minor disturbance, physically, if it is significant. It is important that I now have many relationships with people who are also trying to conduct their lives along these lines, so even when I am not disturbed I am fortifying the commitment to live by different ideals. In the past I was surrounded by people who did not have these kinds of aspirations. At the school I went to people didn't discuss spiritual goals or means or ways. In general these ideas are either unattainably esoteric or unappealingly sentimental. In this program we can have clear spiritual goals that have an evident function. That is what I need, it is probably what you need, and I suggest it could be the genesis of a new way of being.

Step 10 Exercises: Watch out for fucked up thinking and behaviour and be honest when it happens.

Step 10 is a step like 4, 5, 6 and 7 (possibly also 8 and 9) that you take on a daily basis on the hoof. You use the same grid on p272–3. And you also explicitly use the guidance of a mentor.

I often hear people talk about Step 9s that go awry and am quietly and conceitedly satisfied when they reveal that they didn't use the most basic protocols, like doing it after the first eight steps. Whilst there are many ways to interpret the 12 Steps (look on the internet!), there is also an orthodoxy.

Step 10 is the acknowledgement that our previous nature, our previous tendencies, our previous plan will, when we are inert, reassert itself. If we do nothing we will drift back to the old plan.

This step is a troubleshooting tool.

When you fuck up, as surely you shall, inventory it, tell someone else and do what they suggest. If you do all that in your own head, without pen, paper and guidance, it may work sometimes but you mustn't be surprised when it frequently doesn't. By not following instruction but instead relying on our own judgement we are reverting to our core problem, self-will.

Here are some considerations:

- Am I committed to daily growth? How do I demonstrate this?
- Am I prepared to live a truly awakened life and to be alert to the inevitable deviations that will come?
- Am I willing to hold myself accountable to another human being whenever I am disturbed?
- Can I be self-compassionate and trust in my concept of a Higher Power?
- Am I willing to make amends whenever I cause harm?
- Do I consciously try to live a life contrary to the defective impulses that previously governed my life?

11

Stay connected to your new perspective.

Step 11: We sought through prayer and meditation to improve our conscious contact with God *as we understood Him*, praying only for knowledge of His will for us and the power to carry that out.

In active addiction I am disconnected. That is one of the defining characteristics of this condition. I look to reconnect, to recalibrate by using drugs, alcohol, technology, sex, food, domination or some other external stimulant. This is an individualistic and egocentric way to be, the horizon of my inner life made up only of objects to pursue for personal fulfilment. In Step 11 a large part of my life becomes prayer and meditation. This means I am detaching from external activity and seeking a different kind of connection.

To put this in the everyday, I often wake up and immediately feel, before even opening my eyes, kind of glum and anxious and deficient. One negative thought can quickly follow another. I have to intervene in this process. I do it through prayer:

> '*God, I humbly ask that you direct my thinking today, show me how I can be useful to the addicts who still suffer. Show me how I can be of service, how I can be patient, tolerant and kind.*'

Even in writing this now I can inwardly wince at the sincerity. I am accustomed to irony, distance and intellectualism. I am a product of my age and culture. To approach the intention of the prayer, or syntactic inner code reset, if that language is more up your alley, I see that its content is the exact opposite of my tendency when active in addiction: 'God, I humbly ask that you direct my thinking today' – 'There is no God, there's just me and my needs and my feelings and I bet they don't get met. Humbly? Fuck that! I'll be crushed. Be useful to others? Screw them. You make your own luck in this world, do it to them before they do it to you, in the words of Terry Molloy.' Patience, tolerance and kindness do not come easily to me until I retune my mind, and that's what prayer is. Never mind all the wailing, genuflecting and beseeching, unless that's your thing, I suppose. And why not? Embrace the theatre. What I need is to guide my consciousness away from patterns of thought that are deeply ingrained, unproductive and painful. The meditation part of the equation is equally necessary, otherwise I spend all day engaged in the world and its people and opinions. I enjoy having a quiet space inside myself in which peace and serenity are not contingent on the behaviour of others. This step obviously contains a caveat, 'praying only for God's will for us and the power to carry it out'. Prayer will be of little use to me if I summon the power of the spheres and dark matter simply to get myself a new bicycle. Use this new relationship with higher consciousness to acquire the commodity we all need, especially if we are unaware of it: purpose.

To demonstrate the power of this program, my need for it and my faith that it can work for anyone – even its most mystical aspects – I'll tell you what happened the last time I really needed it. I use this program every day. It is my inner referent and my sanctuary, my guide, the point to which I return whenever I am in doubt. But there are times when I really need it, when I am reminded that at its genesis this program is designed to stop people drinking themselves to death. It is a program that works in crisis and crisis is always coming.

The geological layers of soil, then rock, then magma of my self-exploration are as follows: layer one as the shovel breaks the soil, I am an addict, a drug addict and a chronic drinker that will guzzle and down chemicals to keep myself alive. Beneath that I grip onto sexual behaviours and food, compulsion, obsession, greed and lust. With these exposed, uncovered and surrendered to a system, then obsession with work, money, power, the addiction still present but as we go deeper it finds subtler forms of expression, socially acceptable, legal, endorsed even. A deeper look reveals that all the relationships in my life have been artfully if unconsciously constructed to maintain the unaware state of active addiction, codependency in 12 Step language which can be understood as relationships with blurred boundaries or unexpressed, unclear needs and obligations. While in the sweet inferno of fame I gathered a tribe to walk the circles with me and only as I awaken do I see how each relationship was an expression of an unaddressed need in me.

What are the relationships that define you? Who is doing what for you and what do you do for them? Are these relationships an expression of your attributes or your flaws? Likely both but where are you heading and what is driving you? In the language of Arthurian myth, 'Who does the grail serve?' Is your relationship with your partner or your mother a canvas for inadequacy or an unexplored dependency?

My experience is that each layer of addiction as you encounter it contains a lesson within it and the lesson is usually taught with pain. The idiom for awakening in 12 Step language is 'a rock bottom' when there is no further to fall. I have experienced, with varying degrees of severity, the sense of unendurable crisis in each domain of my addiction. And pain is pain. Your pain is your pain, whether you are in cinematic misery or drab slow unremarkable woe; your pain is your pain.

The last time I felt a personal nadir, a crisis, a need for the deep power of this program was in my most recent lap of a familiar circuit of pain. Thanks to the inventorying process I have seen these patterns play out in romantic relationships, familial relationships, work, schools and casual jaunts. There are patterns that I follow when unconscious. It is only when examined through the administrative steps that I get clarity. A quick odd example; in the two of my romantic break-ups which most affected me there were corollaries and themes that were laughable to observe, like an indelible and repeated insignia of personal misery had been continually stamped upon my life. The same problems came up, the same argument with different women. Both relationship break-ups even shared the odd motif of a shared pet at the centre as the sole object of concluding dispute. I didn't notice this until I saw it written down, that in both break-ups I found myself thinking, 'I know I'll be okay, but I'll really miss that cat. Or dog.'

The most important things are too deep and simple for words, they are the province of poetry. In each of our lives these unconscious patterns guide our personal myths. Beyond what I can understand or express in words the symbol of the animal I lost is a coded revelation. In my myth the pet is a totem for that which cannot be said, the symbol has been present for as long as I've been awake. Without examination these lessons go unlearned.

A few years ago in the UK I became embroiled in a general election, mostly through my online expression of my mistrust in the political process. I did a daily comedy news show in which I humorously pointed out hypocrisy and concealed agendas in politics and media. This escalated in popularity and I became involved in campaigns for housing and workers' rights, good causes. At some point though the delicate balance between good intentions and my lust for glory must've tipped because I found myself in direct conflict with media barons and world leaders, the way that a fly might find itself in direct conflict with a rolled-up newspaper.

It wasn't so much the outward condemnation though, or even regret for what I'd publicly said, the outward attacks were from opponents any self-respecting messianic megalomaniac would welcome – Trump, Murdoch, Cameron – and the things I said still stand up:

'The only hope for us, as for any of these protagonists, is to surrender and in so doing fall into the consciousness that cradles all, present in each.'

'Don't vote if there is no real change and unless it's for politicians who will represent people against power.' It was more that, unnoticed by me, like a choking vine around my mind, the pattern consumed my Higher Self. I became seduced by ego and power, by the idea that I could make myself feel better by external means and by plaudits and approval. I now know that other people's approval can't make me and their disapproval can't break me. In the midst of the storm though, splatted on the front pages of newspapers and being discussed on Fox news, I got high. And whenever I get high I am in danger.

When I recounted the tale to Radhanath Swami, a friend and teacher who I often cite, he told me an interesting story. This is the Puranic legend of the elephant king Gajendra as told to me by an American swami, through the dubious filter of my gung-ho autodidacticism.

There was this elephant called Gajendra. He was king not only of the elephants but also of all the animals in the jungle. He was revered and just, but apparently a little bit hubristic, not so much as to put you off him – we're not talking gold medallions, armpit farts and loud drunken anecdotes spoken in your ear at a wedding – more the kind of pride a good-looking but grounded athlete might have. More Gareth Bale than Ronaldo.

Gajendra and his family, which, and I have to say this, included multiple wives – a theme of these tales, I note, is casual polygamy – went down to the lake for a bit of a holiday. This lake was beautiful, but as far as I can gather, also a bit murky and swampy. A fecund and fetid lake, rather than a tipped-out Evian bottle of crystal clearness. In went ol' Gajendra, king of the jungle, for a bit of a swim and a frolic and no doubt to do that 'spray the trunk over the back' move they do at London Zoo. In the midst of this gentle revelry Gajendra was suddenly snatched, legwise, by a crocodile called Makara. Makara sunk his daggery fangs deep into the shin of the elephant king and viced down hard into an implacable and patient clench. The elephant king roared and trumpeted, the terrible treble of the pain rising up through the bass of the rage.

Gajendra fought with all his regal might. Some versions of this tale recount that the struggle went on for a thousand years, the murky swamp curdling with blood, Gajendra's wives weeping on the banks. It is said that eventually Gajendra accepted his fate, surrendered and, breathing his last, plucked from the bloodying water a single lotus flower with his dexterous trunk and held it in humble offering to Lord Vishnu, his God, who in sympathy came and relieved Gajendra, transforming him and granting him access to Vaikuntha, Heaven.

My friend related the story as pertinent because the swamp, or lake, he said, is a territory familiar and fine to crocodiles but not so for elephants. The world of politics, he said, is a swamp and those who live in it are adapted and evolved for such an environment. The compromises they make, the education they have. It is an environment that is good for crocodiles. I enjoyed this story, particularly the opportunity to be cast as a noble elephant king with a harem and I saw how the allegory was helpful. I do not have the training, teeth or hide to easily be in that domain. After eighteen months of thrashing and bleeding I was spent.

But like all good spiritual codes this story is multivalent. In conventional analysis of this myth, the elephant is 'man', the crocodile is 'sin' and the lake is 'life'. On closer and more honest inspection of

> The reason you must tackle your addiction no matter how moderate it may seem or whether it be socially sanctioned is it will, in the end, fail you.'

my altercation with 'the Establishment', I can see how what began as a truthful and noble quest – even if the truth of the quest was to provide people with entertainment and laughter, that is noble – after a while fell prey to my underwater (unconscious) crocodile drive for power and attention. Before too long the crocodile energy is in control, whether it is the external crocodile energy of that forum or the internal crocodile drive of my own avarice. Note the familiarity of the mythic paradigm: Saint George upon his horse fighting the reptile dragon below; Christ on the cross, reaching beyond the human, speared in the side by the armour-covered low-frequency soldier. These stories contain deep truths, like in a dream, like in life, we play every part, the dragon, the elephant, the soldier, the Christ, all these elements are present in our being and the function of these stories is to place us at the centre of our own story, to awaken, to be aware that your unconscious drives can at any time reclaim you and you will be pulled under. The only hope for us, as for any of these protagonists, is to surrender and in so doing fall into the consciousness that cradles all, present in each.

So I slumped, tired of the voices inner and outer. It felt like a familiar point in a cycle, a recognizable despair. I recalled the moment when the drugs stopped working, or marriage or Hollywood. When I could see the tracks before me, upon which I had presumed to run and imagined I would continue running, wrenched up, torn from the soil and suddenly precipitous and vertiginous I stopped dead.

There are reserves we can call upon, secondary habits and modes. At times like these addiction does not come as an enemy but like a mob assassin, as a friend. It places its familiar arm heavily around you and your eyes roll back. When you have excluded a few habits this damascene anguish twists hard. Sleep is the first to leave. Appetite either rises up, a foaming fat and saccharine tide, or leaves you parched and deserted.

A whining need for company, terrified of my own hallways and their sharp shadows. Terrified of my own bedtime. When I stopped doing *The Trews* it swept in from under me. An arrest. A knocked-out boxer cloaked in unconscious self-preservation. I opened up my life like curtains, like a cornflake packet, and I wanted nothing in it. I texted and called another addict. A clean addict. I told him, 'I want nothing in my life. I could walk away from it all. I could put it down like a supermarket basket and walk right out of the store. I could fold my life up neatly on the shore and walk gently into the infinite roar'. I am forty. I am childless. I know that drugs, sex, money, fame, other people, beautiful places, desirable things are all placebos, I've looked inside the capsules. Even apparently worthy causes are somehow hollowed out and I sit in their tin carcass not quite shivering, not quite rattling, not quite knowing what this means.

How does someone like me find their way to faith in God? Do you think I've not read Stephen Pinker and Dawkins or sat through throat-clearing church services or thought, 'This is a fucking ruse, a fucking ruse and a to-do, look at all the golden hats and candles and calligraphy, this is a ruse, a to-do'?

I just stopped. Like with the drugs. I had to stop. They sent me away to a place. Old market towns or coastal towns, places with twee names and brass plaques in their squares and when you see a Caffè Uno there it looks fucking weird and the McDonald's has its logo green, out of cunning respect.

Oh God.

This time, some time spent in Glastonbury. Deep breaths and no deep thinking. Like the first words after a tantrum, all polite. Apologizing.

Through this program you can contact the part of you that already knows what you have to do. Create the stillness for the aspect of your consciousness that knows what it has to do to be heard. We live on a grid, we have a pattern, it runs on primal mechanics. It is hard to pause and reach within to the quiet wisdom, your individual part of the divine that wants to guide you.

'The wisdom to know the difference.' Watch when the 'heat' rises, feel the heat, know that you can intervene. We will always feel the heat of trauma but with these tools we can prevent the negative habits from being triggered.

Interrupting pathology is hard. How can I transcend myself? It's a conundrum. Who is transcending? If I transcend how am I me? Beyond this clanging binary are truths that are hard to render in words, hard even to understand. They can only be experienced. This program contains a mystery. It can be seen as a contemporary tool for conversion, an enlightenment aid. A guidebook for self-analysis, a way of communing with yourself and others. There are I know many ways, the reason I use this one is because it is a simple, efficient way to tackle obsession and compulsion. When my obsession and compulsion are removed, I am a different man.

We've learned to live with shame and pain, we've learned to live disconnected, cast out of Eden. We have forgotten that we can return.

The reason you must tackle your addiction no matter how moderate it may seem or whether it be socially sanctioned is it will, in the end, fail you. Because the drive, the fuel, the impetus behind it is legitimate and its goals are legitimate: connection. In the end it will not settle for a simulacrum. It will be found out. That's why you're lucky if you're addicted to crack or smack, they are fast haemorrhaging, fast failing systems. They provide anaesthetic and distraction but are so bloody medically unsound that they are quickly exposed as dupes. Sex and food can sustain a longer masquerade. Now admittedly you see fewer people hunched over in doorways on ice cream than you do on meth but anyone who knows someone who suffers from an eating disorder will tell you that the sufferer is similarly derelict. And because what we are dealing with is a spiritual condition – a post-religious spiritual calling – the inner condition is what we must address.

When you start to drink, wank, eat, spend, obsess you have lost your connection to the great power within you, the great power in others, the great power around all things. There is something in you speaking to you and you don't understand it because you've never learned its language. So we try to palm it off with porn and consuming but it is your spirit calling and it craves connection. Spend time alone, write, pray, meditate. This is where we learn the language.

The point of undertaking this program, of picking up this book, is to change the way it feels to be in your own head because on some level you don't like it in there. It is making you unhappy. You think thoughts and feel feelings that are unpleasant to experience.

Let's review where we are. We admitted we had a problem. We accepted change was possible. We became willing to learn. We took a good look at the causes of our problems and told another person. We became ready to make changes based on what we'd learned, we petitioned a Higher Power or set a sacred intention to be different. We reviewed the past and committed to amending where we'd gone wrong and then did it if we knew it wouldn't make matters worse.

Then we decided to watch for those old patterns and nip them in the bud when they came up. That is where we find ourselves now: finally ready for a different kind of inner life, a different relationship with ourselves and as a result, different relationships with others. The word for a Hindu priest is a 'swami', which means literally 'he who is with himself'. Implicit in this is the ability to be at ease alone, or in company, settled, not tied to the world by a million invisible strings that can jerk you out of your serenity at any moment.

Before I worked this program I did not spend much time 'with myself'. I did not sit alone and quietly reflect or focus on my breath or upon spiritual axioms. I could sit alone and have a panic attack, or ruminate and worry, or project and fret. In fact that is what happened whenever I was alone so I tried to avoid it. I used to like being alone if I could smoke loads of weed and veg out in front of the TV, or use any drug that slows the mind and creates a temporary chemical haven. When I first stopped using drugs one of the things that struck me most was how profound my inability to be alone was. I couldn't bear it; a creeping dread began to seep under the door like fog if I even envisaged being alone. The company of friends was seldom enough. I wanted the comfort of consequence-free intimacy, which of course meant promiscuity, this behaviour was most tenacious because it is easy to camouflage. Particularly if you have only just stopped taking hard drugs and your sexual proclivities are benign, no one notices or cares. It takes time and self-analysis and a good deal of awareness to reach a point where this pattern can be recognized as toxic and addressed.

I still have a reaction to being alone which is perhaps not entirely natural. A small but discernible surge of fear when I come home to an empty house or when I know my partner will be out. What is causing this fear? Well we now know, thanks to the exhaustive manner in which these steps have been taken, that I have core fears that dominate my thinking and assert themselves in a void. There is no neutral, if I am doing nothing the negative magnetism of my condition will be exerted. If you are new to recovery you can be lenient with yourself regarding solitude. Spend time in the company of people who care for you and that understand you are living differently now.

At my age, both biologically and in terms of recovery, a sense of ease and comfort with solitude is important. This is where one aspect of this step comes into play. 'Sought' is from the verb to seek; I have always been looking for something. I see that now, for as long as I can recall I harboured fantasies of how some object or experience would heal me, would make me whole. Sometimes before Christmas I would be so euphoric at the prospect of the following day's gifts that I'd vibrate until it felt like I might shape-shift. What was I imagining the Millennium Falcon or whatever it was would bring? What was the inherent drive that was so fiercely engaged? I always felt these artefacts would bring completion. It was like I was born with the yearning to be whole and continually felt that each new object or encounter, particularly if enthusiastically heralded, would bring redemption.

I recognize that the innocuous and ordinary Christmas Eve jitters I had as a seven-year-old contained the seed of all future erroneous longing. I can see how easily that became an obsession with food, porn, sex, drugs, relationships, status, money, all objects, mental objects, that prior to attainment can serve as an avatar of salvation. Being saved from what? Being saved from the incompleteness of a life lived within the false structures of ego, maintained by a culture that insists material fulfilment is a possibility. If only you can get the right trainers, the right car, the right girl, the right job, if people would respect you, not reject you, protect you, if you could be like Sophia Loren or Sean Penn or Muhammad Ali or Lady Gaga or thinner or someone else, anybody else, always reaching outwards, always legitimizing the twitching and unfocused drive that will not let you abide.

In prayer and meditation we observe this crackling grid of fast thought. We do not automatically accept this thinking as correct or as a basis for future beliefs and actions. I would not have been able to do that prior to working the first ten steps, my mind was too giddy and restless. Now I am able to sit quietly, away from stimulation, and turn within. My recalcitrant mind churns and gurgles. I bring my attention to my face. Is it relaxed? Usually not, I hold tension around my eyes, jaw and mouth. I consciously relax them. I relax my neck and my shoulders. I move through my body mentally checking where tension is held and releasing it. Once I've done that for a couple of minutes and I'm sure that I'm sitting comfortably, ideally unsupported on a cushion on the floor but not necessarily, I'm allowed to lean or sit in a chair, I move my focus to my breath. I like to imagine the breath being calm and deep, moving through my heart, into my stomach, bringing life. Which is what it's doing, with a few technical respiratory additions. I have been taught Transcendental Meditation, which is a form of mantra meditation where you silently focus the mind on a word, gently and unforcefully returning to it whenever the mind wanders. One consistency that I have observed in meditation is that it is practised with an attitude of self-compassion, that we accept that the mind wanders and don't get put out by it. That we give up any expectation of what meditation should be and allow it to be what it is.

For me it is vital that twice a day for around half an hour, I am not totally immersed in the outside world, whether that's my relationship with my girlfriend or my relationship with my phone. I have always lived in my mind. We all live in our minds and we have allowed them to become poorly tended. Meditation is a way of cultivating the environment in which I spend all my time. When I am on a run with my dog I often totally ignore the beautiful views and the charming antics of my dog in favour of an inner drama of my own contrivance: 'What if this happens?' 'Why did that happen?'

I could be anywhere because I am not present. The state of mind we nurture in meditation begins to inform our whole lives, indeed that is the point. There's little value in Om-ing away at a candle for ten minutes then getting up and bawling out a wayward bin man. Meditation is the cultivation of an ignored and latent aspect of yourself that will cradle you as you re-enter the world of material affairs.

Prayer is, for me, a setting of intention. 'Praying only for God's will for us and the power to carry it out' – this I feel is to guard against the temptation to regard your Higher Power as a cosmic Father Christmas, with nothing better to do than conjure you up a new girlfriend. It also is the acknowledgement that in our former state, prior to reprogramming our mind, the needs of the ego were paramount. The ego tells me I need a new, better girlfriend; I, its ever-willing lackey, go out and get one. The ego tells me I need to pursue fame and fortune; I go tripping out the door in a top hat and spats. This reminds us that the demands of the ego will never lead to anything other than suffering. Desire is suffering. We are free though to relinquish these petty, trivial desires and attune to a new frequency where our life has greater purpose than 'I wonder how I'd look in a new hat?'

This is how I pray. I sit quietly for a moment, I read a few short passages from whatever spiritual book I'm into at the time – at the moment it's Patanjali's yoga aphorisms. I think about how the writing is applicable to my own life, then I silently pray firstly for gratitude. This means I look at myself as a supremely lucky person, to be born in the place, time, health and circumstances I have been, how lucky I have been to have avoided serious injury to myself or others through my past conduct, how fortunate I am to have a life so full of beautiful people. I actually light four candles (!) one representing my personal connection to a higher consciousness as experienced through meditation and dreams, one for my connection to my girlfriend, one for my connection to my work, may it be inspired by high motivation and one for a true connection to all people I encounter. I am reluctant to mention this because it feels both intensely private and also ritualistic and it is both, but I am hopeful that honesty and transparency will connect me to my purpose. Having prayed for gratitude, I pray for courage, a willingness to no longer inhabit my old ways of thinking, not to see the world as a resource for my pleasure but instead the environment in which I can be of use. Then I ask to be healing to people I encounter, that my every interaction is held by a higher intention, when I buy fuel for my car, I talk to the person who serves me in a spirit of unity and love, not as could easily be my unconsidered manner – 'You are here to serve me petrol, that's all I care about'. Finally and perhaps most kookily of all I ask to be shown signs, to be attuned to the world about me, knowing my reality is a dance between the apparent material world and my own consciousness. I ask to be shown the things I need to see, to receive the messages that will help me in my journey.

It is without overmuch emphasis that I tell you that this is an area in which I frequently fail. Most days I lose myself in ego and will, most days the old pattern regains traction. When in traffic, when things move too slowly for me, when I feel inferior or threatened, these newly acquired ways are rattled and tested. This is why I do not work this program alone, I consult others, knowing that I am often not the right person to diagnose my own mental state. A more prosaic approach to this step can be a process of setting plans in the morning and enacting them without being selfish, dishonest or self-pitying. Then at the end of the day to review whether or not you managed it. To be honest about where you 'lost contact' with your higher purpose, where you became once again consumed with resentment, greed, lust or whatever is your poison. This will happen because we are imperfect people whose instincts collide. For me Step 11 is a new conscious connection, a new way, a life that is aware and lived along spiritual lines, a life in which I accept my fallibility and the fallibility of others. It is an intention to live lovingly and kindly, knowing all people are basically the same as me; we are all here suffering together and our job is to love and help one another.

Step 11 Exercises: Stay connected to your new perspective.

The truth is that I am talking to you from the apex of who I am and I doubt I know any more than you.

I am continuing to make amends, my Step 9 is unfinished. Perhaps it may never be. My Step 10s are frequently imperfect. These two admissions perhaps account for my continuing complexity. But I have come, through these principles and the guidance of my Higher Power, a long way from the hopeless junkie I was. Now my problems are the challenges of a man with a truculent brain that tends towards self-centredness who knows that all fruits of the ego are tasteless.

Step 11 is the plain compensation for giving up drugs. By which I mean, part of me just loves getting 'out of my head'. What was that impulse?

Well it was always destructively fulfilled. In Step 11, I get 'out of myself' in a way that is not harmful and connects me to the Great Reality. Consciousness beyond personal psychic and biochemical construction. Or more simply, when I meditate I stop being me.

This is how I practise prayer and meditation in order to improve my 'conscious contact' with 'God'.

I light four candles, one for my connection to consciousness beyond fear, memory, body and senses. One for my connection to my family. One for my connection to my work. One for my connection to other people. I ask that these connections be conducted through love.

I read some spiritual literature, in my case, often 12 Step inspired but other stuff too.

I use mantra meditation to transcend my 'thinking mind'. This is the silent, inner repetition of a sacred word. Sometimes I do guided meditations from YouTube, man, I ain't proud!

I continue for about twenty minutes, hopefully during this time the incessant inner commentary stops and an all-encompassing peace prevails. This takes practice. Be patient and don't judge yourself.

I ask for gratitude and think of ways I can demonstrate it to others. I ask for courage and ways I can demonstrate it. I ask that I be healing to those I encounter. I ask that I see the 'signs' that occur throughout the day that will guide me to my Higher Self, my Best Action. I ask that the thoughts and actions and consciousness that come to me be from a Higher Source.

I repeat mentally three prayers that I know by heart, all from 12 Step literature.

Then I try to stay connected to this peace as I go about my day, in a world awash with provocation and temptation. All through the day, when I want to kick up or kick off, I say 'Guide me, use me'.

In conjunction with Step 10 I check how often I am pulled out of myself and reclaimed by my old ways of thinking, the 'defects of character'. I stay connected to others who are farther down the path than me. I try to remember 'there is nothing to get', 'none of this is real', 'it's only a dream'.

Ask yourself:

- Do I accept that the material and mechanical world as I see it is not objective reality? (Is there stuff I don't know, that no one knows?)
- Do I accept that there is an aspect of my consciousness that is not governed by primal biochemical drives and biographical, social and familial inculcation? (Is there more to my mind than what I've been brainwashed into and what the animal instinct wants?)
- Am I willing to live in service of this Higher Self, this Ulterior Realm? (Do I want to be more than a tangle of greed, need and fear?)

Create your own incantation, your own 'tune-in code' and use it daily.

E.g. *I know I cannot be happy pursuing instinct and will. I devote myself to channelling love, to serving beauty.*

12

**Look at life less
selfishly, be nice to
everyone, help people
if you can.**

Step 12: Having had a spiritual awakening as a result of these steps, we tried to carry this message to addicts, and to practise these principles in all our affairs.

This step is all-encompassing; it comprises a life lived differently, with different objectives, carried out from a different perspective. When I am working this step I am no longer the person that embarked on Step 1.

The three clauses of this each relate to one another. The altruistic aspect of the step – 'carry the message' – in my personal experience often unfolds thusly: a person reaches out to me for help, I think 'I'm not doing that, what's in it for me?' then I realize that I no longer approach life from that perspective and agree to be of assistance where possible. Then I find myself, for example, in a prison talking about drug addiction and I think, and sometimes say, 'The person that I used to be would not have done this, he was too selfish. I on the other hand am doing it, therefore I am not that person.' Usually I don't mention that 'used to be' could refer to a time as recent as that morning. In my working of Step 12 is the understanding that I will always default to self-centredness; if I don't work on my mental and spiritual state I automatically become selfish and indifferent to the suffering of others. A friend of mine says, 'The spiritual life is like rowing a canoe away from a waterfall, if you stop rowing you are pulled backward.'

My condition will always lure me back, back to sex, drugs and selfishness. With Step 10 we can spot the thinking habits that will likely lead back to these destructive behaviours before they take hold. With Step 11 we maintain a state of serenity and connectivity that means these harmful patterns are less alluring. In Step 12 we commit to a different way of life and a different reason for living. In this step is the confirmation that the point of this process is to induce a spiritual awakening, that our problem was living in an egocentric and self-centred prison and that our new motivation is the desire to help others. This still startles me. The one thing I've always been pretty certain about is that this life is all about me. Me and my feelings, my causes, my hopes and dreams and triumphs and failures. For better or for worse, usually worse, I am the protagonist of this drama and, by God I'm going to make it a hell of a show. This unsound mental foundation always leads me to familiar destructive behaviours. This I now believe is because at my essence, the place in me that remained untainted by the decades of self-abuse, I always knew that self-centred pursuits were hollow and diversionary. This knowledge is our true home: it is from here that we feel the resonance of heroism. It is from here that we empathize and love. It is to this ever-present inner sanctuary that we yearn to return. How ironic that all my addictive behaviours seemed so unholy, so carnal. Hedonism and decadence, propelled by the certainty that only pleasure is real and there is no meaning beyond. In mitigation I offer that outside of quaint tales and obscure religion the world told me again and again that this was so, that all that matters is what you can get, what you can control, who you can own. My experience though refused to verify the myth of my culture: the fame did not fulfil, the sex did not fulfil, nor the money, the glamour or the evanescent power. None of it could get inside to where truly I resided, within I remained alone. 'The road of excess leads to the palace of wisdom,' said Blake, Morrison agreed, and I tried to comply. But the wisdom is that there is no 'palace' and that the road of excess has led you nowhere and it's time to go back home.

The 'spiritual awakening' is that I cannot live only for self, the carrying of the message is serving others when they need it, the 'practise in all our affairs' is the final bone-hard, set in stone, small-print, big-impact, 'no way out' clause. Somehow the people who composed these steps knew that those who came after would sabotage their own salvation, and that we'd leap out of the lifeboat and back

'What I used to think of as happiness was merely distraction from the pain. The pain of disconnection, of separateness from you.'

into the sea of illusory suffering any chance we got. Pick up the pipe again, back in the same old relationship, one more drink, I'll leave the job next year, I'll start my diet tomorrow, tick-tock, tick-tock, chisel poised. We need the pain to remind us, the ego is a subtle foe, the Higher Self gives us peace of mind and the ego takes the credit and sends us back into the wilderness.

The awakening that I have had is 'to be happy I must have purpose' and that purpose cannot be any of the things I've already chalked off my long list of indulgences. Sex, food, prestige, power, money or pleasure. We can try and rationalize it, why not, even though I sense the 'reason' may lie beyond liminal comprehension. There is no 'me' – when I say 'I' what am I referring to? My memories and drives, my mental projections and beliefs? My car? My toenails? All dust and spent energy, an impending funeral and then a decade or two of anecdotes in the occasional chats of other doomed trainee corpses. My separateness, my 'me-ness', is not going to provide much comfort then, and a life devoted to the fulfilment of the drives of this odd and temporary conglomeration I'm steering, is no more than the combing of a cadaver's hair. In silence sometimes the thoughts and yearnings abate and there is no 'I' but consciousness continues. This I observe only when the meditation ceases and the 'I' resumes. Could it be that this consciousness is universal? That the field of consciousness that houses my individualism houses yours too? Is this what is meant by we are all one? Is this why when I am kind to others, I feel peace and ease, having reached beyond the boundary of the corporeal and into the unbounded, back to the infinite, back to my home? To overcome the hardwiring of the biological machine in which my consciousness is enshrined is no easy task, impossible in fact for me unaided, but in communion with you I am reminded that the self was never real; that we are all one and undivided, a rolling and unlimited ocean of being, awakening and forgetting, rising and falling with the tides of our lives, happy only in unity.

What I used to think of as happiness was merely distraction from the pain. The pain of disconnection, of separateness from you. All longing, all yearning, all thirst, flung on unworthy surrogates, false idols, unsated by unworthy objects, still pulling us unwillingly back together.

Lord knows I don't want this to read like the rantings of a street-preaching lunatic but you know the game is up and these are the days of change. The old ideas have failed, the temple has fallen and the banks are broken. All these brick and dust structures though are a projection of a deeper thing and it is with this that we must now commune, safe in the knowledge that we aren't walking away from anything real.

Right now at the annual retreats of the world's biggest organizations executives with global power are openly confessing the failure of the old way. They are weeping for their wounded hearts, they are crying out to be brought back home. In rain-spattered provincial towns, beaming and lovely students shine through the small-town gloom as small sums are raised for a barely significant shelter for the destitute. Both deal with the same truth: the way of the self leads only to suffering, the way of love is salvation.

Me, with my proclivity for grandiosity, I will always favour sweeping change and grand revolutions, wild and wordy statements of intent, martyrdom and marvels. This though is the time for humble offerings, for silent acts of loving defiance. The love is the defiance.

Become what you are supposed to be, unbounded, hack through the erroneous codes of your malignant program. We defy them through our kindness, we defy them by reaching out a hand in love, we defy them by loving them, by knowing there is no them. There is nothing to get, there is nowhere to go, that only love is real and we prove this with our lives.

Now, cards on the table, I do believe there is a Higher Consciousness within us and without us and that if we are connected, and doing this program is one way of achieving this connection, then we can commune with it. That is the supernatural, sceptics would say superstitious, belief that I have and I suppose is a defining aspect of many religions. As this is what I have personally experienced it is the only version of the program that I am qualified to pass on, but as I have continually reiterated, my grammar and my understanding of this are personal and individual and yours should be too.

'A Higher Power of your understanding' is a phrase that prevents doctrine and liberates us from circuitous discussion. We all perceive reality differently, we all inhabit our own sensory system, we all imbue the same words with unique and particular meaning. When it comes to a Higher Power the only requirement is that it is beyond your own ego and it isn't malevolent. My earliest conception, in my reluctant and struggling early days, was simple: I was able to stay clean by regularly attending 12 Step groups and by accepting the principle that I could not drink or use one day at a time. Those two things combined were my only conception of a Higher Power and they were enough to achieve what had, until then, been entirely impossible: I stopped taking drugs and drinking. I myself forget, and you will never know how monumental this was. Drinking and taking drugs was all I did, all I cared about and was the means by which I tended to the pain that defined me. The transition from taking drugs on the 12th of December 2002 to not taking drugs on the 13th of December 2002 represents such a significant movement that power of some kind must've been used to achieve it. The eerie fact that, one day at a time, I have not drunk or used drugs since then is easy to categorize as 'evidence of a Higher Power', certainly a power that was not present or utilized prior.

There have been times when I wanted to drink and take drugs. As you can tell from reading this, difficult thoughts and feelings occur daily. I am in constant negotiation with my previous condition. When I have faced serious challenges in recovery the program has been at its most powerful. This is when I know to surrender, that I do not try to navigate my way out of personal pain using the maps I have drawn up myself. I use this program. I have access to kindness, empathy, companionship and experience when I connect to others I walk this path with. I use the inventorying tools to better understand the characteristics and roots of my distress. I am able to alleviate fear through prayer and meditation, the continuing knowledge that my life is not just my engagement with external phenomena. Perhaps most importantly I make myself available to others. I am a mentor; as I've explained a mentor is someone who takes you through the 12 Steps, who has themselves done the 12 Steps, obviously. I mean I wouldn't trust a Sherpa who at the foothills of Everest said, 'Well I've never been up before but I've a hunch we'll be alright'.

I have a mentor myself and a group of trusted people with more time than me that in instances where I am fearful or agitated I can consult with, and importantly, listen to. I value their input above my own instinct. If my instinct is telling me to leave my family and become a monk in the Himalayas (with that Sherpa from the last paragraph) and they say that is a bad idea and that I should remain a householder, I surrender my own idea in favour of theirs. Very simple but invaluable. No point in having a Sherpa (why am I so obsessed with Sherpas? I've no plans to go mountaineering) then, when he suggests a route up the mountain, barging diagonally past him. Knowing that there are people that look to me to guide them through this program has several advantages. For one thing they are all as self-obsessed as I am, so when they call up to talk to me, I am jerked out of my narrow tunnel of introspection and thrust into the busy metropolis of their lives. I listen to other people talking about the challenges they are facing and crucially the insane things they are doing, or if they're good mentees considering doing (they call before they do it), to cope with the condition that we have in common. This condition of disconnection. Neither is the counsel that I offer them just grabbed like a gawping salmon from the babbling stream of my mad mind, no, I listen carefully to what they are saying and mentally consult this program for a route out of the madness. If you're getting advice from another addict and it isn't coming from the program, then you're listening to a junkie.

I am as mad as they are, as mad as you are, often more mad, let's face it, but I am not using my own barmy bible as a guide, I am referring to the principles laid out here, as I understand them. When doing this my self-centredness, the core of my condition, is alleviated because I am being of service to another, which is the much-needed antidote to my type of madness and I also hear myself speak sense and think, like a real dumbo, 'Hey I should do that too!' When I hear myself say to a mentee, 'Well, looking at porn isn't going to make you feel any less lonely or any more valuable,' it is difficult to put down the phone and pull down my pants without feeling a bit ridiculous. Consider the Greeks (oh go on): they talked of 'humours' and 'deities' and 'furies' that would possess and direct the heroes of their myths. Joseph Campbell says that when we are enraged or gripped by jealousy or lust, these supernatural energies have us in their grasp. When I transfer my attention from my own life and problems to the life and problems of the person on the other end of the phone, I have to, and this of course must have a biochemical component, wrench my thoughts off one circuit of the psyche and access another. Attention and intention are the Sat-Nav and petrol of consciousness.

To take someone through the steps properly, as you can see from this book, is time-consuming. Step 5 in particular is a labour of love. There you sit, hour after hour, listening to someone else talk about themselves with no intention other than to help them. Well hang on to your hats folks, but that is not the way ol' Russ used to roll – if I was listening to someone talking it meant that we were about to have sex or they were going to give me some money. Now as I sit listening to some poor old sod unpack their life, like they've been selected for a random search at an airport, I am plugged into my neglected compassion, my empathy, my kindness. To feel these forces awaken within is for me to be reborn.

To be available to people who really need you, to be there 'to carry the message to the addict who still suffers', is to know a new purpose. When I am around other addicts like me, who are on the other side of this program, at the dog end of this disease, I feel gratitude for my own good fortune. I could not get clean, my life was getting worse and now I am free from active addiction, one day at a time. What a relief. The literature upon which these movements are founded describe it not as a 'cure' but as a 'daily reprieve'; the disease, the condition, is still there, you will feel it move through you, in fear and rage and irritation, beckoning you back into your previous behaviour. This can only be averted by continually working this program, in this case Step 12, 'to carry the message to the addict who still suffers'. May I say, in my self-centred life, in this self-centred world, this edict is indeed revolutionary. Where else are these values enshrined? Where are they practised? Only on the fringes. When I meet people who work in homeless shelters or refugee camps or hospitals I feel like I'm meeting saints, and in a way I am because they have stepped outside of the values of our culture and committed to another path. I'm sure there are NHS A&E nurses that are selfish arseholes, I just haven't met any of them. Whether we are discussing the individual or society as a whole, these values can no longer be peripheral, they must become central.

So, 'having had a spiritual awakening' – that means you've woken up to the reality that you and your thoughts are not the centre of the universe, they're not even true and if they're not making you happy – it's time to let them go to make room for 'new thoughts'. 'We tried to carry the message to the addict who still suffers' – we are kind to people now and try to help them, rather than looking at them as lumbering flesh vending machines that might be able to dispatch a little parcel of pleasure if we put the right penny in the slot. 'And to practise these principles in all our affairs' – in our family relationships, our marriages, our jobs, our cars – we now try to be thoughtful, compassionate and kind. Very simple to type, not so easy to live by. Impossible to live by perfectly but we at least have something to aim for now and to try for the rest of our lives.

This need not be done in Jerusalem, this is better done where you are now. Within. Or maybe in Slough.

The Slough homeless centre has a broad clientele. There is a surprising sense of community. More than community. Family. Living cheek by jowl, they quarrel, smile and scowl in Slough. Young homeless kids are addicted to 'spice' these days, an ever-amending and amorphizing packet of crackling pain. One step ahead of the law like the Joker, this readily available legal high is cheap as chips and just as bad for you. The young men are whippet-thin and perch on a teetering plinth of leisurely violence. Tender boys. Girls with fun candy-coloured hair, presumed sex traders with every vein brought to the fore, even those in their faces. Polish blokes who look SAS ready to go, clear veneer varnished hardness. Hard to reach them, hard even

> 'Gruffy, who you hear about before you meet, is a high-status homeless man. Longevity is part of it but his legend reaches beyond his years. His fortitude and constitution hit you as hard as the smell. Although the smell is generic he is unique.'

to be sympathetic, their hardness and my prejudice collude to collide and conclude that they are built to withstand suffering. Survivors, not dislocated, adapted. The shops round there reflect the needs of their clientele, as I suppose all shops do, Polish lagers with jagged names spiked with consonants line up on the shelves of Sikh-run shops.

Me and a few friends from my 'don't drink' gang went down on a Saturday to make ourselves useful. In the kitchen a Hindu group are doing their thing, the same thing, being of service and we carefully avoid a Judean People's Front moment by not insisting they fuck off and help another day. Instead we focus on fellowship and music, a mate of mine Kane brings some well-intentioned musicians and they play loudly in the corner of the shabby and municipal, cracked lino tiles and scraping school chairs, canteen. The Hindus do what Hindus do and serve up aluminium bowls of salad and curry to the unsmiling and intense Poles, caustic candy-haired girls and washboard-stomached and filthy fingernailed boys. My friend and contact Vicky lured me in with her soft hard manner that those women have, those women that have known the streets and known defeat and known men and still dress in grey jogging bottoms and have the unhurried confidence of lags on wide landings.

Gruffy, who you hear about before you meet, is a high-status homeless man. Longevity is part of it but his legend reaches beyond his years. His fortitude and constitution hit you as hard as the smell. Although the smell is generic he is unique. An intravenous heroin addict and Tennent's Super drunk, or whatever the Polish equivalent of Tennent's Super is. Though he himself is British as only service veterans are. The money where your mouth is patriotism of people who would've died for it and now sleep outside for it. You'll only get what they're willing to give you, that's how it goes with the homeless. Gruffy's act is tight. Warm growling colloquialisms that roll out, well, gruffly. 'Alright Guv,' he says; the strangle of vernacular holds you at arm's length. He's charismatic too and the candy tops and the washboards buzz around chipping in with lines from his legend. 'He's on licence. He can't sit down within ten miles of Slough. He's on licence. If they catch him with booze, they can send him down, no court case or nuffin. He's on licence.'

'What's licence?'

'Licence is when they can nick you and bang you up without trial for breachin' conditions.'

Gruffy doesn't react to the telling of his tale, the novelty has worn off. He has been homeless for a long, long time, too long for years and numbers, homeless for tree time, planted, straight out of the army.

Desperate people of course reduce you to a commodity. This we all do in our usually subtler way. What can you do for me? For an addict as honed as Gruffy the transaction is crystal clear, give me a score. I am grateful to be of service, that is why I'm there. With the objective achieved, the two of us still seated, something happens. I eat just the salad and Gruffy does whatever he does instead of eating, probably drinks or pushes a too-tightly wrapped sweaty baguette into a too-taut backpack. But neither of us goes anywhere. And I, high on Christ, the Christ that you find around suffering the connection that we can achieve when suddenly the universe is bare because there on suffering's stage, we know for absolute certain that time and space go on forever and just as surely the body dies. Still seated, we hold hands. And the tears come into his eyes and they are tears for both of us, tears for us all. In them the pain is distilled.

Decamped to an outside smoking area made out of trellis timber like you'd see in a garden centre that, for all we know, was erected by service users under supervision as part of a scheme. This unlovely oasis of one cramped office, modest kitchen slicked in chop grease, sitting room come waiting room, homelessness is constant waiting, a shower room, a few loos. Upstairs a few 'conference spaces' I don't know who's conferring and a store of donated clothes. A lot of denim and not enough socks and pants. 'Underwear is what they need most,' says Vicky, opening the door to a particularly shit Aladdin's cave of third-hand treasures. 'People feel funny about donating pants.' Why I wonder? The intimacy of the garment, a ball-cupping, fanny-clutching reminder of our commonality, the 'there but for the grace of God' ludicrous horror of their plight.

Out under the smokers' trellis where one banned lad orangutans and climbs like vine we gather. 'He can stay if he behaves,' says Vicky and he grins his Lemony grin within his grimy, lemony top. His girlfriend reports to me of his madness and kindness as he coils about and a further crowd gathers, sparking up roll ups and crap brand fags. Not Marlboro lights, I can tell you that. Naturally and necessarily attention turns to Gruffy's legend. His service in the Falklands, his inconceivable time homeless in Slough, his prison sentences, his unjust licence that makes further incarceration inevitable. A choice between whether to walk or stand on an airport walkway.

'Show him yer legs Gruff' says Lemony, momentarily sedentary before embarking on another vertical crawl, and Gruff obliges. One knows that one is engaging in true horror when the sense most offended is not sight but smell. As Gruffy unpeels the nicotine-coloured bandages wound in uneven wads and clods around his shins the stink rises in plumes like liquor and the crowd reel with voodoo astonishment like Americans regaled by David Blaine. As we reach what would once have been skin the bandage has to be picked out like an unwanted ingredient revealing at last a swirling and dreadful crème brûlée of ulcers and craters, each brimming with wet and gentle pus. I'm trying only to breathe through my mouth to avoid the smell but aware that I'm eating whatever molecules I'd've been smelling from this ghoulish buffet of dead flesh. 'Addiction kills,' I think, 'it is eating his body even before he's vacated it.'

Still vaguely euphoric with the electricity of altruism that's buzzing around and trying to stay attuned to holy signals which I believe are present when I'm not tuned into 'up me own arse FM' I decide it is my duty to clean Gruffy's wounds. Actually I think it may've been my mate Nik's idea to do it, yep, I'm pretty certain it was his idea but I don't want to diminish how plugged in and saintly I was feeling amidst all this godawful suffering so let's just say, it was my idea. Me, Nik and Lemony heroically head to the shops to buy supplies, the things you'd buy to clean severe leg ulcers if you knew very little about cleaning severe leg ulcers. Fresh bandages, gauze, white spirit-type stuff, plastic gloves and the three of us march round the aisles in Slough Boots like avengers.

We stop in a Sikh-run Polish booze shop to buy Gruffy and a couple of the others a few cans. I've never been one to impose abstinence where drink and drugs are clearly needed. It's not for me to judge what a street-sleeper does to cope with their inexcusable suffering. I think that compassion and understanding even in this dubious form provide more comfort, hope and are even more likely to inspire change than impotent piety and unresearched judgement. Or as Bill Hicks says, 'Damn right this money is for drugs. Drugs are pretty important to a drug addict.'

On departure I holler at Lemony to hurry up in some overly familiar way and he offers me out on the spot 'I don't care if you are Russell Brand', he says, 'I'll fuckin lay you out.' I say nothing but secretly think I could probably do him because of all the spice and my recent Jiu-Jitsu classes, though in retrospect, it would've been bloody unpleasant and would undermine the crusader element of our day's work there. Also people with nothing to lose are in my experience formidable opponents, even if they are quite skinny. What I'm saying is it's probably for the best we didn't have a fight.

Streamlined lives these Slough addicts have. Refined to a needlepoint of pain. Once Lemony and I have addressed our moment of conflict, which amounts to me apologizing for hollering at him across the SHOC forecourt while he does pull ups in the doorway of the offie, we head back, a shambling cavalry. This young man who is clearly a handful, capable of being a dick, sleeping rough and up for a ruck, is enthusiastically focused on this first aid mission, motivated solely by an intention to help Gruffy. A clear, altruistic objective. In this moment as we bound back from Boots, all three of us are working a program. Three addicts at different points on our journey, in this moment elevated above our differences by a simple goal. We extract Gruff from the forecourt fags and fetch one of the aluminium salad bowls. We decamp to a conference room upstairs, me, Nik, Lemony and Vicky. Gruff folds onto a plastic chair and we close the door in on us. As we haul his jeans up above the knee and start to unravel the bandages the smell steps up its game. Like the previous smell was sunlight and this smell is the sun itself, a scorching source of pitiless stink. I wonder what it'd look like if you could see it. Big.

Vicky is a professional and was herself homeless, Nik too has served time in a hedge, Lemony is still an outsider so I am very much the Fauntleroy in this rescue op and so have to keep myself at the forefront to avoid looking a ponce. We've barely unravelled a leg

> 'I don't know if I'll ever return to using drugs or drinking or promiscuity or the selfish pursuit of money and reputation but I do know that when I live my life, one day at a time, and follow a simple program I am a more whole and useful man.'

when Nik (again!) decrees that this job is too much for us and that we need a doctor. Looking at the shin surface which is like a bubbling alien swamp it's difficult to argue. Gruffy is of course drunk. Not drunk like when a non-alcoholic is drunk, which has an air of Conga line wackiness to it, no, dutifully drunk, drunk as his neutral, drunk as an ablution, like combed hair, but still he's behind a wall of booze, then the wall of cracked pride that resigned people have. Like he's faraway, down a well.

He's not mad keen to visit a doctor either, let me tell you, because, presumably, of a total mistrust of institutions, and who can blame him. If I'd spent my twenties dodging bullets on Goose Green for Thatcher then came back to Blighty and wound up homeless in Slough my sense of trust in authority might dim. More than that though I sense is the thought that trying to solve this problem is futile. So many rancid layers to unravel and pick through, so much accretive pain that Gruffy likely feels it'd be easier to move forward to the grave than to turn and face the change.

As we ease the reluctant Gruff into my nifty Mini, along with Nik and Bear, oh yes, I've got my lolloping German Shepherd with me, I watch how my mind reacts to unfamiliar stimuli. As we know, the core of the addictive condition is self-centredness. I recognize this diagnosis. I seamlessly inflate natural self-interest and self-preservation into an imperceptible (to me) but all-encompassing dominion of self-obsession. All I think about is what I want. I begin to see the world as stuff that is either useful to me or not useful and react to it on that basis. This doesn't feel as selfish as it sounds while I'm doing it. For example while living my life through the continual prism of sex addiction, which in my case took the form of heterosexual promiscuity, I wasn't aware, and would have denied if confronted, that I had no real concern of the impact of my behaviour upon the women I was sleeping with. That doesn't mean my conduct wasn't kind or affectionate and it, from an external perspective, never crossed any meaningful moral boundaries, but in actuality I was consuming the experience as a distraction and a sedative in an obsessive and compulsive way that I was unable to transcend or witness because it occupied the seat of my consciousness.

It was only over time that my feelings of guilt and emptiness, coupled with a growing sensitivity to the emotional harm being caused to the people I was having sex with, was significant enough to challenge my previous perspective. A perspective that is culturally endorsed. In a mechanical model, a materialist model, 'a single man has sex with consensual adults' has few practical negative consequences. There are a few: disease, infidelity on their part could lead to an altercation. It is only when one advances the condition of a Higher Perspective that the behaviour is not only challenged but entirely unravels. If you have a mechanistic world view – that 'a human is a type of biological robot and its brain a kind of computer' – the introduction of a morality that has at best evolved as some kind of *Sesame Street*-style 'let's cooperate' social glue is a blunt tool in the unending face of limitless space. Even atheistically the humanist standard to which one appeals when arguing for notions such as 'right' and 'wrong' seems muddled. In a dualistic humanist model right, or good, is no more intrinsically valuable than wrong, or bad.

Somehow, through moderating my interaction with the material and sensual, I have come to personally know a different type

RECOVERY

of consciousness that seems kind of close to what Shakespeare, Augustine, Mohammed, Siddhartha, Martin Luther King, Gandhi, Rumi, Jesus and a few thousand other thickos and conformists refer to as 'God'. Bear with me. These are secular times. I just went to see a priest with my girlfriend to discuss getting married in his church and God wasn't mentioned, as if doing so might cause embarrassment and I feel some of the same tension when writing. It's not like the atheists have all the best tunes, though some people who I really admire are devout atheists, but it is the time we live in, the mechanical dome that umbrellas us from the eternal that causes me consternation. The unwillingness to open our hearts to the mystery. Even a sentence like 'open our hearts to mystery' makes me feel a bit queasy with its sincerity but nothing has given me a stronger sense of the great unknowable than listening to scientists, some spiritual, others not, confessing to the limitations of understanding being through material analysis.

I (like the saints and sages and prophets on my earlier list of heavyweights that this time I'm too shy to repeat in case it seems that I'm trying to edge myself onto the inventory of greats, which I am) feel there is some other power at work here. I feel too that in my journey to freedom from active addiction, undertaken basically for selfish reasons, I have inadvertently been connected to this power. I also believe that anyone can do it. That is what is at the heart of this book, that addiction, however severe or mild, is a sincere attempt to address a real problem, the lack of fulfilment to which the material world cannot cater. Therefore the solution to this problem is a spiritual connection. This is not my idea. It might be Carl Jung's idea or AA founder Bill Wilson's idea. The fact is that it doesn't matter if you are gambling to the point where it harms you, if you are drinking too much, if you are lost in your life and afraid to articulate even to yourself how unhappy you are, how fearful of the future, of death, of other people, of being poor, of not being good enough, sexy enough, thin enough, tough enough, famous enough, if you feel that you are not enough and that if you could only 'X, Y, Z, then everything would be fine', I believe you are on the spectrum of addiction. By this definition: 'Trying to solve an inner problem by outer means, in spite of negative consequences'.

My qualification is that I have, like some almost inconceivable idiot, put this drive, this want, this need, to work so many times – I've tried to solve this feeling of emptiness, dissatisfaction, worthlessness at various times in my silly little life with chocolate, heroin, showing off, masturbation, becoming famous, money, crack, getting into exciting relationships, getting into politics, self-harm, puking up, rage and frankly Mr Shankly it's been a carousel of absolute bollocks. As in those bloody analogies that annoy you in the first line, the thing was inside all along. But here's an annoying analogy anyway, as told to me by my highly evolved spiritual friend and rival in self-help literature, Radhanath Swami, and by God am I paraphrasing: 'There's this type of goat, a musk goat, that earned its name by stinking of sheer, unadulterated gorgeousness, this goat is highly prized by the perfume trade (the bastards) as a few drizzling squirts of this musk it has in its glands, once extracted, blows the bloody lid off a titchy bottle of Paco Rabanne or whatever. The musk goat (or deer, I can't remember) spends its whole life sedulously trip-trapping around treacherous mountain paths and getting its fur snagged in thistles (and possibly getting cross-bowed in the shank by Calvin Klein) in its determined and lovelorn pursuit of the source of this most bewitching fragrance, when in reality all it has to do is stick its snout up its own bum. Or wherever the musk gland is. So, you know, the source of this long-sought contentment is within.'

Now obviously there's more to it than that or this would be a very short and unprofitable book. Ultimately though the contentment, excitement, distraction that you (like a goat that would've been better off felching itself) have been pegging on anything from drugs, to jobs, to the perfect boyfriend is attainable by attuning to a different aspect of your own consciousness.

I don't know if I'll ever return to using drugs or drinking or promiscuity or the selfish pursuit of money and reputation but I do know that when I live my life, one day at a time, and follow a simple program I am a more whole and useful man. Part of this program, an integral part, a part that in the pit of my belly, when off-kilter, I seethingly resist, is that I must make myself of use to others. In this instance the 'use' is as a driver and the 'other' is Gruffy. Nik is back seat and I'm cautiously driving us to Wexham A&E while I guess at what music Gruffy might be into. I seem to recall this fiasco ultimately undertaken to the score of 'True' by Spandau Ballet. It's a hot day and Gruffy's legs are cooking up nicely, but at least he's not cooking up smack as we wheedle down country lanes on our way to an underfunded casualty unit that he doesn't seem that into visiting – I know this much is true.

In spite of, no because of, this escalating inconvenience, I am 100 per cent in the moment and not thinking about myself at all. I am committed to this little mission of getting a rowdy veteran to hospital. It's as if the transfer to a car has, to Gruffy's booze-addled brain, translated as a kind of *Beano* and he seems pretty fucking jolly actually as he joins Tony Hadley in the chorus. 'This is the sound of my soul.' I fucking hope so Gruffy.

In the pupae of privilege that the last ten years became I seldom visited NHS hospitals and so am not that well equipped to deal with the car parks and barriers and rules and 'Don't park there it's an ambulance bay' humdrummery but I do my best, knowing that once the Spandau is over we have to get Gruff into an institution and that's where the real ballet begins. Nik and I deal with the early administrative duties, after the mandatory waiting time, during which I feel grateful for the things in my life which stand between me and Gruffy – parents who love me, a girlfriend who loves me, sobriety, a good job, a home, health, clean clothes, teeth, shoes, pets – it's a long list and yet there is a connection. When I pause and look into his eyes it is clear that the essential differences between us are few and insignificant. It could be boiled down to luck. Unexamined hubris is easily indulged. It is very easy for me to think there is a merit to my circumstance, sometimes I still think it: 'Didn't I do well, against the odds, getting clean, overcoming humble origins, becoming a famous entertainer'. Then I pause to remember how each of those details was actually arrived at. How the story I have in my head about reality, my own reality, is in fact constructed, not fictitious or deceitful in a vindictive way, it is more that I have conjured up a version of reality that suits me.

In the plastic bucket seat of Wexham A&E Gruffy goes in and out of what passes for consciousness in his wasteland of addiction, decay and pain. He is autonomously undertaking this process, having very much handed his will over to Nik and me, the providers in this instance of the necessary motivation to confront the cutaneous symptoms of a magma-deep problem. Every so often he stirs and threatens to leave and Nik and I vie to be the most buoyant advocate of bandaging. It is kind of parental I suppose and hopefully loving. Each interaction with a member of staff is a hair-triggered affair where Nik and I carry Gruffy's gelignite nature like a tray of badly stacked crockery. The first fella is merely taking a few personal details and Gruff still dispenses the occasional spray of *bons mots*.

It's funny to see the world through his eyes. He is an odd conglomerate of life and death. The severity of his plight a distillation of all our lives. Death is coming, life is hard, what shall we do? The interaction that jars most is when we are shown via a patronizing but necessary and helpful colour-coded route to the purple zone where Gruffy gets his blood work done. The Romanian nurse (I think?

Could that assumption just be because she's taking blood?) is a bit too green, fragile, thin-skinned to deal with Gruff. At the points where he lifts the veil of his screensaver persona, 'Alright Guv', he is frightening. The pain that he is cloaking is the pain that drives men to murder. His eyes change, his jaw tenses, his drab compliance is suddenly shed, shabby jowls lift to bear sharp fangs and I wonder if I'm qualified. If being a do-gooder is what's required here. But being of use to others is part of my program, especially to those that share my condition. How then do you navigate the complications such an edict throws up? Gruffy is scary and potentially violent. Never face a using addict alone – you are outnumbered, the addict plus their disease, plus your own disease versus you. So Nik and I are doing this together. How do you stop yourself from milking the situation for spiritual credit? Of course there is no such thing as spiritual credit, as soon as credit is sought you are in the domain of the ego. So even by writing about it the purity is compromised if not undone. How do you avoid making it about the result? You just do your best and let go of the outcome. It's easy to become snared on each of these points. In the end, you just try your best.

The nurse keeps rooting around with a needle under Gruffy's skin trying to find a vein. It's like watching a trailing molehill ruin a lawn in a cartoon. No luck on the left arm. Gruffy curses and Nik and I are gently restraining him and offering phatic pleasantries. He's taken his jeans off at this point. They have an organic quality to them, wet and dry as if the death in them is residual, used-up life, like compost. The nurse walks round the gurney to try her luck with the other arm as Gruff, now fully into his cantankerous mode, mumbles trash talk and says, 'I'll find a fuckin vein,' and the nurse seems a bit harried. She clambers around under the skin on the inside of his right elbow as if trying to retrieve a phone from the shallow gap beneath a sofa, when eventually Gruff's taunts get to her and she says, 'I can't do this,' chucks her works in a yellow bin and leaves the curtailed space.

In what will become a well-worn trope Gruff reaches for his living-jeans saying he's had enough and Nik and I try to pat down the intermittent flames of his impotent rage. I feel simultaneously sorry for and pissed off with the nurse. Sorry because of her hard, underpaid, overworked, underappreciated job and pissed off because she didn't treat Gruffy right. And before I can accept that my role is not to judge but to try and be of use, the perfect Maccam nurse bowls in. She's built for the job, stout and foghorn-voiced. 'Used to be a screw,' she says as Nik and I marvel. She incongruously refers to Gruffy as 'Dude' and handles him with assembly-line elegance. There is a timbre to her voice that alters his entire manner. 'Okay dude. I'm gonna needya to takeya jeans off and sit on the bed.' Gruff opens his throat to send up a flare but – 'I'm here to helpya dude, sit back on the bed pet.' The easy authority of the wing and barracks fishhooks our man and places him tenderly but firmly back on the bed. This is what's needed I think, recalling my own first brush with tough love. My then agent, with his love so tough it didn't seem like love at all, just like intense eye contact and a smack in the mouth. Someone who stood between me and self-destruction and self-hatred, not like a mum or a nan, with tears in their eyes, no, with a '*no pasa nada*', 'that's enough out of you sunshine', 'sit down, before I knock ya down' authority. Which is one of the neglected and beautiful traits of masculinity. Not exclusively male of course, but perhaps it is in the male domain where its absence is most felt. This nurse, who I'm pretty certain was called Sheila, had it. Gruffy settled. She had a whole department to take care of so she soon departed and left us on the conveyor belt with Gruff's blood undone and we awaited a doctor. It took a while.

Nik and I do shifts with Gruffy. Alone with Gruffy I ask how he found himself on the wrong side of the apocalypse. A living tapestry unfolding in real time of loss and pain and sadness, of life on pause. I ask him not to call me 'Guv' but to call me Russell, in my mind this will hoist the curtain that he's cast between us. But like unpicking the bandages, unpicking the past is painful for him. Perched on a hospital bed, in a stupid backless gown with a pointless faded floral print on it, his little legs dangling. He tells me about a wife and kids and a life seventeen years ago. He tells me about life in the forces, sort of. But his communication is veiled. Perhaps because of my own inability to deal with intimacy, which is really just reality, I turn on the camera on my phone and film him. He clocks it but carries on and a sudden frustration blurts forth and he says, 'So many times I've tried to end it. To finish it', he mimes injecting his neck so aggressively, punching himself in the throat, self-destruction so literal it's awkward as well as awful. Then he coughs so deeply it's like he might die so I stop filming. Here I feel the hopelessness he lives with, I am sold. It is futile, there is no way back, there is no point in dressing the wounds. Fuck it, let it rot. What can I say to him, 'It'll all be alright mate'? I think that's probably what I did say but here I am struggling to understand. I don't understand. I suppose it isn't my job to understand, my job is to be compassionate and loving and offer hope, not to evaluate and assess like a spiritual chartered surveyor or an Auschwitz attendant, the value of a life, the chances for a life. Be kind.

Nik comes back on duty at this point and actually does much better than me at chatting to Gruff. At one point when I'm striding about the ward, trying to be noticed to entice a doctor or nurse or someone, I hear Gruffy laugh behind the curtain. The two of 'em are in there, partitioned and actually having a laugh. I feel a bit jealous that Nik got a laugh out of him but mostly happy that a bloke that moments ago I was ready to write off as a corpse is now enjoying the craic with another drunk on the other side of the curtain. When a doctor does come he is more in the first nurse camp than the second and irrespective of the hours spent, which I see as invested and he sees as wasted, Gruffy regards the doctor's wafting sweetness and professional air as a trigger for departure.

A friend of Gruff's, Chris, his partner in churchyard slumber, is in the waiting room, the whole world is a waiting room to them, and the pair ultimately settle for twenty quid each and a trip back to Slough, my little car jammed with tramps, surprisingly upbeat. As we disgorge them at the roadside, other lads from the SHOC facility are there waiting and in spite of what would seem to have been, for all practical purposes, a total waste of time, everyone is rather jolly. Perhaps because they have some money in their pockets to score? In my experience though, drug addicts of the distinction we are discussing do not skip to the dealer's like giddy debutantes, it is a functional business.

In the coming days a mate of ours who was also there at the Slough shelter, Kane, an ex-Royal Marine (roll that phrase around your tongue like wine why don't you, 'An ex-Royal Marine' – imagine!) hangs out with Gruffy and verifies through military channels Gruffy's military history. He arranges for Gruffy to meet with a charity for ex-service people, in London on the Monday, and the future opens up for our man: this charity offer grants for living and accommodation – 'Everything is going to be okay!' Sure, we didn't get Gruff's wounds bandaged that day but, look now, lady luck, through an angelic ex-Marine, has smiled down on Gruffy and he has a chance of a new life after seventeen years a slave in Slough. On the Monday morning Kane shows up at the SHOC centre to meet Gruff and take him down to London, sadly, inevitably, Gruffy is 'in no fit state' to get on a train. Still unready to unwind the bandages and look at the wound. How is this then a demonstration of the power of recovery? A tale about nearly helping someone. For me it is an example of a group of drunks and drug addicts that have been granted a way of living free from their addiction, attuned to a new frequency. Simple kindness, a willingness to help others, lifted me that day out of the familiar pit of self-obsession, I felt useful and worthwhile, I felt connected. I felt inspired by the kindness of my fellows and grateful to have been spared the suffering that Gruffy endures. I feel too that there is hope, that this resource, this Power that is within Nik and Kane, is within us all and if we are willing to let go of old ideas of what life is and what happiness is, a world awaits us that is more beautiful than we have the power to imagine.

Step 12 Exercises: Look at life less selfishly, be nice to everyone, help people if you can.

Having had a spiritual awakening as the result of these steps, we tried to carry this message to the addict who still suffers and to practise these principles in all our affairs.

Well, there's no going back. Having surrendered, admitting we have no power and can't cope, coming to believe things could improve if we could connect to a new source of power, handing over our self-will, inventorying, confessing, being willing to let go of deep, negative patterns, committing deeply to real change, making a list of people we've harmed, making amends where appropriate, keeping our eyes peeled for a return to old ways, staying connected to this new awakening and powerful consciousness we now, finally, discover that we have to dedicate our lives to helping others and being loving in all areas of our lives.

It's a long journey. Sometimes when watching US domestic policy around healthcare being enacted or UK financial criminals being rewarded, I am reminded of my own imperfections. I too am selfish, I too am greedy. What would be nice though, I reflect, is not to build a system of world governance, on these, the most destructive aspects of the human spirit, which also includes sacrifice, kindness and altruism. These are the hues of the human palette that we wish to see worlds rendered in.

Step 12 is a commitment to live in accordance with the Higher Self that we discover while undertaking the preceding steps. We may never be perfect but perfection is our aspiration. To become the most beautiful version of ourselves that we can possibly be. To build a life, a family, a community, a world, on spiritual values. This is less grandiose than it sounds. Step 10 and 11 keep us aware and plugged in. Step 12 ensures that we are doing good works. That we do not revert to the old idea of life, that our life is a pit that need only be filled with pleasure. That if we decide to follow this way, we need never be afraid, because we have surrendered our personal aims. We now live to be connected, awake and of service. When I wake up, I tune in. When I go out, I know I will be challenged.

- **What are your motivations right now? Is it to get something? Prestige? Power? Glory?** *Yes. A little bit. I hope this book is a major success and people will say 'Wow, that Russell Brand, what a great guy, he found a way of making spiritual principles accessible to a whole new demographic.' But I am aware of it. I am continually asking to be shown how to make this book of maximum benefit to the most people.*
- **Have you done anything for anyone else today? Especially without being 'found out'?** *Well a few little things, nothing major. I'm going to go to a 12 Step support group later and I promise I will conduct my service (that means do some admin that I've volunteered for) lovingly and I will reach out to my mentees.*
- **Have you meditated and connected?** *Yes. But not as well as I would've liked because I've been fretting about getting this book finished.*
- **Well, have you called anyone else for help? Have you prayed?** *No, but I will.*

This program is simple and it works well with complex people. It ̶ ̶de up of ancient but timeless principles: overcome the ego, co ̶ ̶ Higher Self, a higher purpose and serve others. Step 12 is ̶ also a spur to remind us that our work is never finish ̶ journey of discovery and service and each of us h ̶ realize and an intended self to recover.

Consider:

- Have I experienced a deep change in my thinking, feeling and behaviour?
- Am I willing to share my life to help those I encounter?
- How can I particularly help others?
- Do I balance my life between helping others, self-care, relationships and work?
- How can I improve?
- Do I put this program before all else?
- Do I transmit this new life, this recovered life or my old ideas, my old egoic plan?
- Do I continually ask that I may be useful to others?

13

Re:Birth

Laura had been so pregnant for so long that any other state seemed inconceivable. I watched the house fill with subtle signs of a new arrival, a pram, tiny clothes and I myself participated in the painting of the baby's room but it all seemed like an abstract and ceremonial exercise.

Something we were doing as a blind ritual of appeasement. I looked at the robust and ridiculous pram in the hallway and said to Laura, 'But where will we go? When would we ever need such an object?' She did not enjoy the line and in fact became annoyed. I just couldn't think what use a pram would be.

I don't know why the world persists with the idea that a pregnancy lasts nine months either when it plainly lasts for ten and by the end of the ninth the waddling goddess does little but beseech the tardy heavens for delivery of this inconceivable cargo. Quietly I said my own prayer, I asked for preparedness knowing all was about to change but not knowing how. The change from not having a baby to having a baby is too radical to be taken in one almighty leap. It should be handled in instalments, like those magazines where each edition is accompanied by a further piece of the Cutty Sark or a Spitfire (issue one 99p – 'I hope the second issue isn't a fiver!'). The baby should arrive one foot at a time. An ankle independently issued, then a finger or an ear, the mouth last. If I can take care of this leg successfully, like a girl at an inner-city comp lugging around a bag of leaking and battered sugar, then I can take the rest of the infant in a few months. Instead the whole incredible bounty arrives in one opera of glorious revelation.

3 a.m. Friday the 4th of November 2016. 'Russell,' says a voice through the silence and the stillness. 'I think it's started.' I know of course that

this is a signal of commencement, a call to arms, the starting pistol has been fired but as a prospective father I do not know what manner of race is to follow or where the finishing line might be. When we awaited the result of the seven-week scan I relayed my concern to a friend: 'What if there's something wrong?' 'Even if there isn't,' she said, 'then you have the twelve-week scan, the thirty-six-week scan, the birth, the childhood, the adolescence. You're a hostage to fortune now.'

'I've been awake since midnight, the contractions, or surges, are eight minutes apart.' We call them 'surges', when we remember, as the medical language around childbirth is negative and unhelpful, we learned on a course called 'hypnobirthing', which may as well have been called 'hippie-birthing' because that's what it is. I get up and I think put the kettle on and move some towels around, having some semi-conscious recollection that this is what the situation demands. What I sense though, on the periphery of my awareness, is that a greater force is about to be asserted, reducing all of our human activity to ornamental incidentals.

We use an app, of course, to measure the contractions in the half-light of our bedroom. I take this extremely seriously as it is the only job I have. I try to press the timer at the exact moment that Laura says 'Appy', the regrettable safe word we agreed for a contraction, sorry, surge, commencement. Our cats move to the pinnacle of their individual characters. Morrissey, in his high-street tux, stands impassive and intense, a centurion of our tiny kingdom. Jericho, all Bengal exoticism, flits and leaps and asserts light-footed diagonal scrambles across this newly sacred space. Downstairs, the Bear, the big brown Alsatian, sighs. This time moves most magically. Laura seeking out new places to stand and breathe and fall within. Me observing and dreaming up duties and wondering which particular sounds might signal a need for departure, or any kind of action. They, the midwives, tell you that when the contractions, sorry, fuck, surges, are one minute in duration and three take place in a ten-minute period it's time to go to the hospital. The app, or 'appy' though, doesn't see it that way. After every surge, meticulously tapped in by me, a message pops up on screen: 'Time to go to hospital'. Of course our bags are packed for the trip. Snacks and blankets and laminated pages of high-minded instruction. The problem though is that the difference between a 'drill' and the reality is always so distinct as to render all but the best preparation useless. The bags lie dormant in the spare room like a sepia postcard from another man. The other man was me in the past, a me who had only hypothetical challenges, whereas this man, me now, has to contend with the universal 'Great Challenge'. I put the bags in the car, which I had filled with petrol some days earlier. How can the mundanity of preparation ever truly steel us for the drama of the event? Our rituals must call to mind a deeper truth; they must be a portal to the future and the past. A connection. No time to think about all that now though, I have to get back upstairs and tend to Laura, who is, I believe the technical term is, from the carol 'Away in a Manger', 'lowing', as in 'the cattle are'.

It is this intervention of a greater, previously concealed nature which provides much of the substance for the remainder of the labour. Laura, my serene, kind and thoughtful girlfriend, who supports and takes care of me with such grace, is becoming a mammalian hulk. An animal, a goddess and very definitely the epicentre of this situation, and if I may be so bold, of life itself. Because ultimately, what else is there? I 'call the midwife'. It is 6.30 a.m. now, she grapples snoozily with the phone and I can hear pillows and half-light in her voice. 'Laura is having contractions,' I say. 'Surges?' she corrects. 'How far apart are they?' They are between four and six minutes apart. We are instructed to call later.

In our room the magical intimacy remains. Real specialness. Not like the Baftas or a John Lewis advert, but a daunting sense of impending wonder. It is in the synthesis of the physical and divine that I find myself frozen in astonishment. This is plainly about the body, about pain and muscle and groaning and blood and dilation. What though is this secondary element? This sense of being held, guided, carried, if not by a metaphysical grace then by the pathway already walked by all of our ancestors. This is the path in essence, from unlife, to life.

After a few more meticulously observed and diligently timed hours of lowing and leaning and occasional gentle exclamation and one ill-advised attempt at yogic chanting by me (obviously) we summon the midwife, Karina, a South African, apparently this is mandatory, and she arrives and is pretty cool. Towels do seem to be necessary; it's not just a cliché. More necessary in fact than a male presence so somewhat crestfallen, I go for a run with the dog. There's a good deal of politics in the childbirth world, did you know that? There is a plausible feminist theory that childbirth has become unduly medicalized in order to transfer the power of the process from women to men, from nature to technology. We learned a lot about this over the pregnancy, hence words like 'surge' instead of 'contraction', terms like 'special circumstances' instead of 'complications'. Some of it seems a bit hippie, even for me as a bloke with Hindu symbols tattooed on my arm. Other aspects, like giving birth on all fours, not on your back, in darkness, not under an intrusive medical light, and in your own time, not at the behest of an obstetrician's schedule, all seem spot on to me. The role of the male in all this is of course, secondary and I, due I suppose to love and the transcendent magnitude of the situation, find in myself the inverse of Laura's potent warrior life portal, a kind of gentle silver service butler bloke, whispering and popping off to get ointments.

Not far into the run I check my phone and Laura has called to say come back. The process has sped up and once I've clomped back through the fields with breathless portent I return to the bedroom and Laura is indeed on all fours, waters broken or 'realized', 'released' actually and the whole place has that kind of moment after fire alarm or bomb scare atmosphere of studied calm. Karina says we should leave now or have the baby in our bedroom, which I am totally down with but Laura is the boss so off we go, her couched up in the back next to the currently vacant baby seat mooing and crowing and all sorts, in a beautifully unselfconscious way.

I sit up the front, chauffeuring us through the country lanes, sometimes having to go real slow when Laura surges, trying to work out how I feel about the midwife being in the car because I'm kind of touchy about strangers. We get to the John Radcliffe Hospital in Oxford and go via the giant aluminium lift, pasted with posters of local events and activities for the staff to do while Laura leans and moans and different orderlies and nurses and other people who see this sort of stuff every day just go about their business. And I feel protective, like I want to wall her in. It's odd to feel protective when there's probably nothing to protect someone from, you're kind of being protective in a bubble. It is an evolutionary anachronism. I feel like a kangaroo, or iguana making some once vital move, now redundant in the busy, lumbering lift. We get to our floor, the seventh, and buzz for entry to the midwife centre and I feel self-conscious about Karina, like we've brought our own bourgeois mechanic into a Kwik Fit. The indigenous midwives eye our interloper like alley cats.

We are taken to an assessment room and Laura, who is super no nonsense and irritable at this point, gives short shrift to Marie the Latina midwife who wants to check her out. We left the house because Karina said Laura was 3cm dilated. This Marie, on inspection, disputes and it feels a bit like a courtroom drama where the vying sides call independent experts to validate their positions. 'It's subjective,' says Marie, 'we all have different-sized fingers.' It is about 11 a.m. and she tells us she'll be back to check on us at about

4.30 p.m. as she leaves. Karina clearly feels like she's shot her load a bit early by bringing us in and Laura and I are both disappointed that the ceremonial and mysterious atmosphere of our room has been replaced now with the sterile and pragmatic plainness of the hospital. I also feel aggrieved at the loss of intimacy and the supplanting of the natural with the bureaucratic and I think Laura feels the same but of course her vocabulary is severely stunted by the groans every few minutes and the agricultural gloom that she now displays.

Karina goes to the hospital shop and leaves Laura and me together. I am, I'll admit, a little sulky at this point. I am desperately trying to wrench my head out of self-centred irritability and into my necessary role as supporter and protector but I just feel really pissed off that we've driven away from Eden to come to what feels like a kind of barren and inferior environment. I feel like we stopped listening to our instincts, our higher selves, in this instance a rare fusion of animal and angel, and instead subjugated ourselves to procedure and now we are being punished. 'If you trust in God, God will carry you, if you abandon God, you're on your own.' I feel alone and disconnected and am trying desperately to retune myself, to refocus on the woman on the bed, going through her first labour. I reach into the bag for the laminates. They contain a script for me, written by Laura, in anticipation of this moment, the moment when we are in the early part of labour and unclear of what to do, and I revert to type, insular, *lost in self.*

What I am evidently meant to be doing is coaching Laura through her breathing and keeping us connected and in the present. Thank God for these scripts I think and throw myself into character. My solipsistic and neurotic fears focus on something being 'wrong' with the baby, ranging from stillborn to birthmark, I shuffle through the endless deck of potential disasters that could befall me. 'Replace fear with faith,' a friend of mine told me when I'd mentioned it to him.

> Labour is defined by nature. Laura is its central deity, moaning, roaring, birthing and we the secondary cast reach unwittingly into our own deeper selves. The women are more experienced and vie for matriarchal dominance. I, the lone male, an innocent, prowl and wait and serve. I have been relieved of the self-centredness of the previous hours and can now feel the rhythm of the drama.'

I do this now and am soothed. Laura, through the groans and after an impromptu and again very animal shower (like when Greenpeace workers douse a beached dolphin), tells me to WhatsApp her friends and the prospective grandparents. I do this. I send pictures and succinct 'social media' style aphorisms. Laura is possessed. Not by an external entity but by her truer nature, she is possessed by the person she needs to become: a mother.

Finally we are invited to choose another room to move to. Marie has decided, based on the quality, cadence or something, of the sounds that Laura is making, that it is time to decamp and asks which room we'd like to water birth in. Laura decrees from her hands and her knees on the gurney that we will have the windowless room and we waddle off, through some tarpaulin membrane across the corridor, evidently work is being done and this adds to the feeling of transition.

Once in the birthing room, with its pool, which is a big bath, its rolling purple, pink and blue lighting and cavernous, intimate solitude, things start to improve. I now have a few jobs. I can fetch things, yes, but also I am monitoring the lighting. Turning off all but the psychedelic swirl. Laura, encouraged by the change of scene, goes into a new, more intense and focused mode. Karina is now a comforting and reassuring female companion and there are fewer skirmishes between the Jet and Shark midwife gangs. Just one actually, about turning the tap on. Marie is territorial. Labour is defined by nature. Nature is near. Nature is with us all. Laura is its central deity, moaning, roaring, birthing and we the secondary cast reach unwittingly into our own deeper selves. The women are more experienced and vie for matriarchal dominance. I, the lone male, an innocent, prowl and wait and serve. I have been relieved of the self-centredness of the previous hours in the previous space and can now feel the rhythm of the drama. The beat behind the skin and voices is asserting itself. The pulse, the life, is seeking its dominion.

Laura moves into the water, lit like a Hendrix album. On all fours again she pushes and I watch aquatic roses of blood gently bloom behind her. This excites me but Marie checks Laura's dilation and says she's only 5cm and we must be 10cm before pushing can begin or Laura will haemorrhage. Although this seems serious and there is much talk of Laura's blood group and, insanely, samples are taken, even during contractions, I feel now that we are going to be alright. The beat is louder now. Something else is present.

Here I see the power of Marie, the unshakeable certainty of a veteran. 'Laura, when you want to push, you take the gas and air. You inhale and you exhale into the tube. You do not push. Very important you do not push. Do you understand?' Laura, naked and perfect, does understand. It is maybe 4 p.m. and the contractions are more frequent and one comes on now and I pass the gas and air and she falls into it. I watch enviously as Laura levitates. After the first blast she becomes yet more holy, inhibitions exhaled, a sense of immersion and self-realization of which, along with the free buzz she is inhaling, I am quietly envious of. 'These women know what they are doing,' I think as I resume my job as an orderly.

Marie especially is totemic in her efficiency. These women live in proximity to drama, to life and birth and death. She had battlefield calm. I feel the irritation I always have when I sense I am near incompetence dissipate. She is in and out of the room incessantly and now and then you hear women scream and babies cry and dramatic though it is, it remains secondary, a scoring to the central events of our private and personal theatre.

Laura swirls in the water and sound, and they all become as one another, nature is but one thing. Divinity is in connectedness.

An hour or two of this 'don't push' business and Laura asks Marie, 'When can I push?'

'When it is totally irresistible. When you can't not push.'

'I think it's irresistible now.'

I observe this perched at the poolside, holding the gas and air, occasionally pouring water on Laura's glistening form.

'Can you feel inside yourself?' says Marie. 'Put a finger inside yourself and tell me what you can feel.'

'I can't reach very far,' she says. 'There's something there.'

Then Marie, with a gentle, perfect, only just perceptible smile: 'Something solid, with hair?'

Odd, that given the context Laura genuinely doesn't seem to immediately equate this presence with the emerging head.

'Yes,' she says. 'I can only reach my finger in to here,' and she indicates the first knuckle, just after the nail, on her index finger.

'Laura,' says Marie quietly but with a kind of entirely new but somehow familiar wisdom. 'Now you can push.'

A contraction duly arrives, Laura pushes and roars. Screams and contorts her face. Amazingly she doesn't swear but uses Enid Blyton curse words like 'golly!' and 'gosh!', and a melodic and beautiful wailing, it is like siren song, here she is, in water, crying out in primal pain with harmony, harmony with herself, with the sound, with birth. Marie and Karina have now put aside their minor tribal differences and join the harmony. They move round her supporting her position, counselling. I am kind of at a spiritual and primal football match. I have none of Laura's syntactic restraint and am vacillating between 'FUCKING HELL! Go on Laura!' and long and gut-felt 'Aum's'.

Laura wants to be in a different position. The contractions, surges, fuck, surges, are near constant now, she swishes about in the pool, on all-fours, on her back then finally squatting, like a frog on her toes, heels up, knees outward and we lock at the eyes and the forearms. Laura here dives within herself entirely, as clearly as if physical fathoms were sought, she deliberately goes within. The pool is raised so I am able to see Laura's vagina perfectly and my eyes dart between hers and the true focal point of the action and in this moment the midwives seem like corner men in a prize fight, hanging back, knowing now that coaching and strategy are over and only nature remains.

I can see the mound of the head, round and burgeoning behind the vagina which is not yet open. Laura somehow manages to be completely primal and well-bred simultaneously, finding a voice I've never heard before but still not swearing. There is but one moment of doubt amidst this giddying climax. 'I can't do it,' she says to Marie, who responds, again with the barely perceptible smile, 'Laura, no one in the history of mankind has not given birth after reaching this point.' With this gnostic promise received Laura roars more. It is intense and an aperture emerges, heralded by an unfurling flume of blood, like a silent clarion call, and I see the head. A small circumference, a coin-sized revelation of the top of the baby's head. How can it all be surprising? How is it so amazing? I mean this is what we are here for, why then is it so amazing? More surges, more roars, more PG swearing. The vagina opens and I can see more head now, I am involved, like a very late, eighty-ninth-minute penalty at Upton Park involved, like life and death truly depended on football.

Then, our arms locked, another push and fifty per cent of a human head appears. It is beyond spectacular, so often spectacle is without substance. Another push, more roaring, both of us now, me effing and blinding and aum-ing, Laura screaming, a life-affirming, animal scream. An instrument to measure pulse is produced, the head is nearly out, the baby's heart has slowed, a few glances dart but we are reassured. 'It's normal,' says Marie, then another push and the whole head, for a moment, just the head, is out. Nature. This extraordinary and vivid sight, this strangeness, a head, lolling below the surface so peculiar but just nature and then the final push, a scream, frozen clocks and stillness. The body emerges and moves not with independent motion but with the caress of the water. Once I tipped a dead goldfish down the toilet and was saddened by the resurrection the water granted. In water the fish rippled in elegant perfection, a momentary aquatic resurrection.

The baby is moving only by the power of the water. The baby looks like an effigy of a baby, a doll, a special effects baby, a model, the motion is provided only by the water. All is so quiet and still. Laura and I both reach down and she takes her. 'It's a girl', the cord trails and tangles. Then, in her mother's arms, with searing and sudden certainty, as if touched by the finger of creation, her eyes flash open and life possesses her and exudes from her. Like seeing behind the curtain as she moves from life's shadow to life. How different is inanimate flesh to a living being. I watched the life flow in and in this moment when she came online, when her consciousness ignited, I felt new life enter me.

I've heard new fathers say, 'I never knew such love was in me,' but I always knew, I just didn't know what to do with it. When I saw her I knew. I knew her and I knew what to do.

I climbed into the pool. Laura talks to her daughter: 'Hello. I'm your mummy. I'm your mummy and you've done so well.'

She doesn't cry but we do. Not sobbing or weeping, tears run as if a newly acquired altitude is wringing them from our faces.

Conclusion

The promises in 12 Step literature seemed absurd to me, almost sarcastic. Too twee, too cute. Forgive my evangelism but I feel I have been saved and that you can be too. More than my outward impecunity I was impoverished of spirit.

What's more, and many who know me well will vouch for this, I am and have been a kind of über individualist, determined to walk my own path, writing my own religion traipsingly with my toes. My dislike of authority and institutions was so entrenched that I would reject even loving guidance. When I embarked on this program I was entirely entombed in brittle wisdom of my own composition. I could not be in the moment and I did not know peace. I was unknowingly devout, believing that if I became a movie star and a prolific lover then I would be free, elevated, absolved. I believed this, I now realize, because I thought that if I was that, a movie star and a philanderer, I would be other; I would no longer be me. In spite of my narcissism, which is undue and unhealthy self-regard, I did not like myself at all.

What began as an opportunity to be free of my most obvious outward problem, chemical addictions, turned into, with very little authority from me, a total excavation of who I am and what it means for me to be a human in the world. I mentor a lot of men, I listen to their mad indulgences and crazy behaviour. Generally I think though, 'Wow, you're not as crazy as me.' I'm not trying to perversely place myself on a podium at an Olympic games for idiots, I'm literally in awe at the efficacy of this program. I am like a former fat man, stood in his gigantic old trousers, two thumbs up and lithe, unable to believe the change. And I am not the architect of the personal cathedral in which I now gratefully repose. It was already there, I was just slumbering outside it, shivering, knowing for certain that I myself would be the one to save my world. Well that's not how it went down. I was freely given a technique that induced a psychic change that worked and continues to work. First it somehow got me free of drugs and alcohol then it gave me a way to be a better man.

If your goal is perfect peace, I think that may only be attained when the lights go out. Perhaps in death there is freedom. But if what you want is a way of being in this world with your drives and our culture's demands then this program will make your life first manageable and then beautiful.

Today I woke up and I did not look at my phone, as my truculent thoughts began their march on me I intercepted them at the gate with surrender, 'I hand this day over, show me how to be of service.' I am staying in the Lake District in a friend's house. It is beautiful here. It is intense and the sky is low and the rain moves sideward across the face of the day. I have a girlfriend with whom I share peace and easy communication. In the room is our young daughter who wakes up laughing. I meditate and set intentions for the day. I suppose I can't be surprised if you think, 'It's alright for some', rather than, 'How did this happen?' because you have been on your own journey and haven't seen mine, and not one step of it hinted at this place as the destination. When I was making polite conversation in crack houses, I did so fearful that I may never know freedom. When I flung myself again and again at the feet of strangers, like they could somehow be an altar, I didn't know that one day my garbled prayer would be heard and I'd be freed. And if for me, why not for you?

We left the house with our galumphing hound, like the dog my dad had when I was a boy, like my ex-girlfriend's dog, a German Shepherd, but I'm free to love this dog knowing that while he may be mortal he is ours, he isn't about to be taken away, as long as I stay faithful. The image of domestic serenity is built upon this program, there is no secret dread waiting to upend it. I have a normal life. I'm not secretly gambling or having an affair. I am what I look like on this walk, a member of a family. Bear being what he is, unruliness wrapped in brown fur, is soon off sheep-bothering and I am now a man in a field chasing a dog, mindful not to impotently holler his name, not to draw too much attention to this clumsiness. The sheep are unharmed, thankfully. Bear is tethered and we wander down to a cafe on Lake Coniston, The Bluebird Café. I of course didn't bring any money and ask if we can pay for our coffees next time and they say it's fine. We sit outside in ordinary bliss and when it's time to leave the wind picks up, and we, as tentative new parents, are uneasy when a group of female walkers move to sit at an adjacent table. 'After you', 'No, after you' and all that. I am secretly frustrated for a second, as I want to use the toilet before we leave and am unsure how to manage – if I take the dog, he'll probably eat someone's breakfast or set off a fire alarm, if I leave him with my family he'll unsettle these walkers – but before I can even properly formulate my anxiety, one of the ladies is joyfully offering to hold the dog and taking the lead so kindly that I am both admonished and reminded that the world is full of love just waiting. And ten minutes and half a mile later Laura and I are leaning into the rain and the baby in her harness is getting wet and again we are about to accuse both the world and ourselves for allowing this to happen when the woman from the cafe, who must be in her fifties, comes running and calling, brandishing the waterproof cover from her rucksack, insisting we take it to cover the baby. She stands in the rain fastening this makeshift baby kagoule across our daughter. Irene is her name and she just couldn't bear the thought of us walking in the rain, she says.

A few hundred yards on, the weather still treacherous, we stop at a gift shop and ask for a taxi number. The fella in the shop introduces himself as Brian, says he knows the house we're staying in because his missus works there cleaning, in fact he'll give her a call and she'll drive us home. What is this world so full of kindness? Where is the world from the solemn TV news? Was the world always so gracious when I sat cursing and abusing? Were there angels all about me then, holding me in my belligerence? Hannah arrives and cheerfully packs us all into her car, our swamp of a dog an' all, and deposits us home with the same easy and human grace that this program took me from my misery and placed me in this life. 'The kingdom of heaven is spread upon the earth and man sees it not.'

'It's alright for you,' you may think again, and I wouldn't blame you. It is alright for me, but it wasn't always so, at least I didn't see it. I felt impounded and hopeless and it all changed. It became this life as if that was what had always been intended. As if some force was waiting for me to invite it into my life, when I was ready, ready to let go of all my illusions of misery and power, potency and shame.

My old way of life is with me still like a worn-down coin in my pocket that I toy with from time to time. Like a madman I sometimes countenance going back, back into the burning past to snatch at some scorched pleasure. The program must be lived completely, consulted whenever my thoughts stray. How did I become this person, on the other side of my misery? On the other side of my life?

I know that life is still there, waiting for me if I ever choose to go back, if I ever think there's something left in the ashes. Even fatherhood would not be enough to hold me here in the blissful present if I let go of my program. Even after the revelation of my daughter's birth.

In chemistry, when two substances are introduced, if either component reacts at all, then both are changed forever.

This program helps us to recognize early when we are transitioning from our 'right mind', a balanced and connected perspective, and into the warped perception of our disease.

When we recognize this we can take action – attend support groups, contact a mentor, do step work, help others – we have a choice, we don't have to wait for the agony to arrive before we take action. If we have a good Step 1 we have accepted that we have a problem and that without a program we will continually tend towards discomfort and diseased thinking. If we accept that we need to work a program, rather than inwardly insisting that 'it's not fair' and 'life should be easier', we are continually reminded, by this defective thinking, that we need to be active in our program or we will be active in our disease.

This aspect of the disease I refer to by many names: 'ego plus', 'the daemon', 'the extra bit of madness', 'magic', 'the edge' – this additional and destructive component that addicts often have appears to reside exactly adjacent to the ego, and the ego covets it. The problems I encounter are often induced by my egocentric reclamation of this 'daemon' magical energy. My experience in Hollywood deteriorated and became painful when I became egocentric. Even though, superficially, it was the fulfilment of a dream. My experience with politics and activism became toxic when the sense of purpose that initially inspired me became, unnoticed by me, appropriated by selfishness, an egocentric drive. This mercurial, impersonal energy has power, and I feel it, in 'my' body, I witness it with 'my' mind, so it's easy to individualize, to take individual credit for. But actually, is there anything for which I can legitimately take credit? I didn't give myself the ability to speak or write. I didn't invent the English language, or the printing press or the camera, or any of these things upon which any success I've enjoyed has been built. This is why I need to be grateful for success, never proud of it, because in short,

I have done nothing. It was all just there. When instead of grateful I feel proud, when instead of blessed I feel anointed, it is a sure sign that I am soon to be in mental peril.

This energy, this mercurial and impersonal power, in conjunction with the personal ego somehow conspires to find a destructive outlet. Perhaps because the 'shadow self', the unconscious and pre-linguistic mind, recognizes that the ego is a barrier between the individual Self and this greater, impersonal power and has to immolate the barrier, has to burn it, discharge it. Perhaps this destructive drive in essence, which we call addiction, or a suicidal tendency, knows that 'I' is not 'self'; that in fact the self has to go, self has to be destroyed for the Higher Self to be realized and if there is no spiritual protocol through which to achieve it, then we have to find another method, behavioural or chemical, to ameliorate the self to give us connection, to give us liberation.

The 'disease' itself is not bad. It is trying to get somewhere, it is trying to take you somewhere, it is trying to free you from the illusion of the individualized, ego-defined life.

I am aware that I only have the life I live now due to the principles of this program and my connection to a Higher Power of my understanding. It is the framework through which I experience reality. It has given me purpose, freed me from trauma and shame. It has given me the sanctuary that I sought from each false prophet that briefly illuminated, then stained, my using life. It has shown me that sex, drugs, fame and money are no more likely to resolve the yearning that I've always felt than porn or biscuits. If you feel that yearning and that you've never quite fitted in this world then you should give yourself and this program a chance because the yearning itself is real, it's trying to lead you home.

The Program

The Program

Here are the exercise questions again, without my answers so that you can think about your own.

Step 1: Are you a bit fucked?

1 What do I want to change?
2 What pain or fear do I associate with change in this area?
3 What pleasure am I getting out of not changing?
4 What will it cost me if this doesn't change?
5 What are the benefits I could gain by having this changed?
6 How has this problem placed my important relationships in jeopardy?
7 Have I lost respect/reputation due to this problem?
8 Has this problem made my home life unhappy?
9 Has this problem caused any type of illness?
10 Do I turn to the type of person that enables me to practise this behaviour or to companions who enable me?
11 What part of the problem do the people who care about me object to most?
12 What type of abuse has happened to me and others due to this problem?
13 What have I done in the past to try to fix, control or change this area of my life?
14 What are the feelings, emotions and conditions I have tried to alter or control with this problem?
15 Right now, if this is such an important area in my life, why haven't I changed?
16 Am I willing to do whatever it takes to have this changed, healed or transformed?

Step 2: Could you not be fucked?

1   Do I believe that I need to change?
2   Do I accept that change means I must think/feel/act differently?
3   Do I know people who have made comparable changes that seem quite radical?
4   Is this change likely to be easy and driven by the ideas I already have, techniques I already use and support systems that I already have access to?
5   What is my conception of a Power greater than me? Is it nature? Is it consciousness beyond the individual? Is it the power of people coming together in the pursuit of a noble goal? Describe your personal understanding of a power greater than yourself.
6   Do I have doubt and prejudice about spirituality and the power of a new perspective to solve my problem? What are those doubts and prejudices?

Mantra
'Limitless consciousness, source of all light and love, please lay aside for me doubt and prejudice and give me willingness to believe that you can solve this problem, too, the way you have solved other problems.'

1   What is my conception of a personal Higher Power? Describe it here.
2   Can I now accept there is a power greater than me at work in this cosmos?
3   Do I know people who have changed their lives and live according to spiritual principles who are connected, happy and real?
4   Is this how I'd like to be?
5   Do I know people who have engaged with a new Power and used these techniques to induce revolutionary change in their way of living and thinking and have found a new peace and direction?
6   Is this what I want?

7 To reiterate, is this how my life is now? Or am I struggling with relationships? My emotions?

8 Do I lack purpose and drive?

9 Am I creating conflict and chaos?

10 Even beyond my primary addictive behaviour (drink/drugs/food/sex/spending/technology) are things hard?

11 Am I getting depressed?

12 Am I afraid?

13 Am I helping others?

14 In other areas of my life have I exhibited behaviours that if repurposed could serve me now? Like for example my belief that I can make myself feel better with drugs or sex or tech or the right relationship or job or some chocolate?

15 Have I kind of worshipped drugs or my phone or sex or shopping?

16 Can I see that this impulse applied to something less mundane, materialistic and shallow may motivate change?

17 In fact this problem I have could be seen as the misdirection of a positive impulse if I look at it differently, couldn't it?

18 Can I connect to this love within me that I sometimes misdirect?

19 Can I connect to the love outside of me that I see in others?

20 Can I connect to this Power that I see elsewhere in my life?

Mantra (put this into your own words)

'Divine Power, Supreme Truth, love within and without, guide me to a new way of being. Help me to put aside all previous thoughts and prejudices that I may be open to a "New Way". I ask the creative power deep within me to guide me towards the person I was always meant to be, to seek out relationships and experiences that will move me closer to this Truth.'

Step 3: Are you, on your own, going to 'unfuck' yourself?

1   Am I feeling unsatisfied, limited, empty or anxious in my
    relationships?
2   Do my feelings lead me to make (or not make) decisions, take
    (or not take) actions, or say (or not say) things that I then regret?
3   Am I suffering from misery, depression, unhappiness, or low
    self-worth?
4   Am I suffering from anxiety, doubt or perfectionism? Am I projecting
    imaginary future scenarios then worrying about them?
5   Is it becoming clear to me that my plan is not working?
6   Is it clear that I need a new plan that is not sourced from my own
    head and drives if I am to find fulfilment?
7   This plan of mine is like a mind virus of self-obsession. Can I
    surrender it? Am I open to a different plan? Am I open to being
    guided?

We are trapped in a way of 'being' that is not working. Here are some
categories which will help us amend our perspective. We can usually
identify the root of pain and spiritual discomfort within these areas.

1   Pride (what I *think* you think about me)
2   Self-esteem (what I think about myself)
3   Personal relations (the script I give others)
4   Sexual relations (as above, pertaining to sex)
5   Ambitions (what I want in life, my overall vision of my 'perfect' self)
6   Security (what I need to survive)
7   Finances (money and how it affects my feelings)

It is good to be reminded of these categories as we undertake Step 4.

Step 4: Write down all the things that are fucking you up or have ever fucked you up and don't lie, or leave anything out.

Use the table on the next page.

1 Where did I make a Mistake?
2 Where have I been Selfish?
3 Where was I Dishonest?
4 Where was I Self-seeking?
5 Where was I Afraid?
6 Where am I to Blame?
7 Where am I at Fault?
8 Where was I Wrong?

I Resent	Because	This Affects My

My Part

Choose which of these are relevant for the third column:
Pride
Self-esteem
Personal relations
Sexual relations
Ambitions
Security
Finances

Choose which of these are relevant for the fourth column:
Mistakes
Selfishness
Dishonesty
Self-seeking
Fear
Blame
Fault *(For a full list of Faults see p81)*
Wrong

273

RUSSELL BRAND

Step 5: Honestly tell someone trustworthy about how fucked you are.

Before beginning this step, ask yourself:

1   Have I been entirely honest in this inventory?
2   Have I been clear about the motives beneath my behaviour?
3   Have I reached into my innermost self and asked for truth to be revealed?
4   Am I open to a new truth?
5   Am I willing to take full responsibility for my feelings, perceptions and my behaviour?
6   Am I willing to fully disclose the most intimate and previously concealed nature of myself to another person?

The person we choose should themselves have undertaken this process and have no investment in our life other than a desire to help us.

Ask yourself:

1   Why am I doing Step 5?
2   Why am I doing it with the person that I have chosen?
3   What is the function of Step 5?

Step 6: Well that's revealed a lot of fucked up patterns. Do you want to stop it? Seriously?

With each defect we identify (from the third and fourth columns), ask:

1 Why do I do this? How does it help me? (What do I want, or want to avoid?)
2 If I do not change, what will happen?
3 If I am willing to change, how could my life improve?
4 Do I want this defect removed? Am I ready to let go?
5 If the answer is 'no', ask yourself: how is my life unmanageable due to my powerlessness to change this attitude/thought/ behaviour pattern?

Ask yourself:

1 Am I willing to let go of my egocentric, self-centred world view?
2 Am I willing to tear up my plan?
3 Am I willing to stop blaming others? To let go of resentment?
4 Am I willing to use this program as the new plan for my life?
5 Am I willing to accept that there are more powerful forces than me in the universe and that in this context my motives and notions are ridiculous?

Step 7: Are you willing to live in a new way that's not all about you and your previous, fucked up stuff? You have to.

Ask yourself:

1   What do I want to change?
2   Am I going to change it?
3   Do I commit to change?

Step 8: Prepare to apologize to everyone for everything affected by your being so fucked up.

Go through your Step 4. Anybody, or any institutions you have harmed, add to a list. The fourth column, 'Wrongs' section will be of particular use.

Then for each item or person on the list note the name and:

1   What I did that was harmful
2   What should I have done instead
3   Who suffered as a result, and how

Once you have completed the list and the above questions you have to ask yourself in each case:

Am I willing to make amends to this person?

Step 9: Now apologize. Unless that would make things worse.

Ask yourself:

1   Am I willing to change?
2   Am I willing to be changed in ways I may not be aware of or in control of?
3   Am I willing to address each harm that I am aware of?
4   Am I being completely honest with my mentor about the nature of the harm?
5   Have I thoroughly prepared each amend with a mentor?
6   Am I willing to complete all my amends using creative solutions for individuals I can't meet?
7   Is finishing my amends a top priority in my life?
8   Have I finished my amends? Am I avoiding some?

Step 10: Watch out for fucked up thinking and behaviour and be honest when it happens.

A written Step 10 can be completed by using the Step 4 table on a daily basis.

Consider:

1 Am I committed to daily growth? How do I demonstrate this?
2 Am I prepared to live a truly awakened life and to be alert to the inevitable deviations that will come?
3 Am I willing to hold myself accountable to another human being whenever I am disturbed?
4 Can I be self-compassionate and trust in my concept of a Higher Power?
5 Am I willing to make amends whenever I cause harm?
6 Do I consciously try to live a life contrary to the defective impulses that previously governed my life?

Step 11: Stay connected to your new perspective.

Ask yourself:

1 Do I accept that the material and mechanical world as I see it is not objective reality? (Is there stuff I don't know, that no one knows?)

2 Do I accept that there is an aspect of my consciousness that is not governed by primal biochemical drives and biographical, social and familial inculcation? (Is there more to my mind than what I've been brainwashed into and what the animal instinct wants?)

3 Am I willing to live in service of this Higher Self, this Ulterior Realm? (Do I want to be more than a tangle of greed, need and fear?)

Create your own incantation, your own 'tune-in code' and use it daily.

E.g. *I know I cannot be happy pursuing instinct and will. I devote myself to channelling love, to serving beauty.*

Step 12: Look at life less selfishly, be nice to everyone, help people if you can.

1 What are your motivations right now? Is it to get something? Prestige? Power? Glory?
2 Have you done anything for anyone else today? Especially without being 'found out'?
3 Have you meditated and connected?
4 Have you called anyone else for help? Have you prayed?

Consider:

1 Have I experienced a deep change in my thinking, feeling and behaviour?
2 Am I willing to share my life to help those I encounter?
3 How can I particularly help others?
4 Do I balance my life between helping others, self-care, relationships and work?
5 How can I improve?
6 Do I put this program before all else?
7 Do I transmit this new life, this recovered life or my old ideas, my old egoic plan?
8 Do I continually ask that I may be useful to others?

Resources
A note on severe addiction issues

I can attest personally that the 12 Steps work with severe addiction
issues, if you have them, you should engage with the appropriate
support group. There are now hundreds of 12 Step organizations
with objects of unwitting fetishization: alcohol, narcotics, gambling,
food, sex, hoarding.

A quick online search will help you find the right resource in your area.
Here are a few places to start:

AA contact details

Alcoholics Anonymous UK
www.alcoholics-anonymous.org.uk
0800 9177 650

Alcoholics Anonymous Australia
www.aa.org.au
1300 222 222

Alcoholics Anonymous New Zealand
www.aa.org.nz
0800 229 6757

Alcoholics Anonymous South Africa
www.aasouthafrica.org.za
0861 435 722

NA contact details

Narcotics Anonymous UK
www.ukna.org
0300 999 1212

Narcotics Anonymous Australia
www.na.org.au
1300 652 820

Narcotics Anonymous New Zealand
www.nzna.org
0800 628 632

Narcotics Anonymous South Africa
www.na.org.za
083 900 69 62

GA contact details

Gamblers Anonymous UK
www.gamblersanonymous.org.uk

Gamblers Anonymous Australia
www.gaaustralia.org.au

Gamblers Anonymous New Zealand
www.gamblinghelpline.co.nz

Gamblers Anonymous South Africa
www.gasouthafrica.wordpress.com

DA contact details

Debtors Anonymous UK
www.debtorsanonymous.org.uk/
0207 1177 533

**Debtors Anonymous Australia &
New Zealand**
www.debtorsanonymous.asia

CODA contact details

Co-Dependents Anonymous UK
www.coda-uk.org

**Co-Dependents Anonymous
Australia & New Zealand**
www.ozcoda.webs.com

**Co-Dependents Anonymous
South Africa**
www.codasouthafrica.co.za

Literature

There is a lot out there but here are some classic 12 Step books:

Alcoholics Anonymous
- *Alcoholics Anonymous Big Book*
- *Twelve Steps and Twelve Traditions*
- *Daily Reflections: A Book of Reflections by A.A. Members for A.A. Members*

Narcotics Anonymous
- *It Works: How and Why*
- *Just for Today: Daily Meditations for Recovering Addicts*

Russell Brand is a comedian and an addict.

He's been addicted to drugs, sex, fame, money and power. Even now as a new father, fourteen and a half years into recovery he still writes about himself in the third person and that can't be healthy.

This is his fourth book. He still performs as a comic and is studying for an MA in Religion in Global Politics. He has two cats, a dog, a wife, a baby, ten chickens and 60 thousand bees in spite of being vegan-curious. He is certain that the material world is an illusion but still keeps licking the walls of the hologram.

Part of the profit of this book goes to 12 Step and abstinence-based recovery causes as part of an ongoing commitment on behalf of the author to help people suffering from addiction-related issues to find a new way of living.

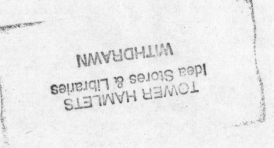